LORA O'BRIEN

Tales of Old Ireland: Retold

Ancient Irish Stories Retold for Today

First published by Eel & Otter Press 2018

Copyright © 2018 by Lora O'Brien

All rights reserved. No part of this publication may be reproduced, stored or transmitted in any form or by any means, electronic, mechanical, photocopying, recording, scanning, or otherwise without written permission from the publisher. It is illegal to copy this book, post it to a website, or distribute it by any other means without permission.

Lora O'Brien asserts the moral right to be identified as the author of this work.

Published by Eel & Otter Press

Dunmore Road, Waterford,

County Waterford, Ireland.

www.EelandOtter.net

(Irish Heritage Books, Blog, Audio, T-Shirts, Mugs)

First edition

ISBN: 978-1722223786

Proofreading by Beth Marshall

This book was professionally typeset on Reedsy. Find out more at reedsy.com

I dedicate these stories to the generation after those we lost...

Saoirse, Ahlanna, Conall.
David, Céilí, Kane, Grace, Tommy, Euan.

"Let the Reader's Voice
Honour the Writer's Pen."

{Marginalia}

> Unknown Medieval Scribe
> (recorded in the margins
> of a manuscript)

Contents

Foreword iv
Preface vi

I The Mythological Cycle
About This Time... 3
The Guardians 5
Black Birds 8
The True Tale of Tailtiu 11
The Union at the River 15
The Brush and Comb 18
Lugh at Tara 23
The Harper 26
The Children of my Sister 29
The Crooked Bloody God 32
The Sorcerous Sisters 35
The Wheel 38

II The Ulster Cycle
About This Time... 43
The Three Sisters 45
The Great Queen 48
The Curse of Macha 51
Amergin and Ellen (not a love story...) 54
River Woman 57

The Sorcery of Scáthach	60
The Pillow Talk	65
The Prophetess	68
The Cave of the Cats	71
A Form Very Excellent	74
In the Alps	77
Getting Well	80
Snow White Skin	83

III The Fenian Cycle

About This Time...	89
By His Thumb	91
The Ninth Wave	94
The Sidhe at Keshcorran	97
The Magical Deer	100
Fionn's Feast	103
The Red Haired Hare	106
The Hearth in the Hall	109
The Fairy Lover	112
The Hurling Hero	115
The Mothers	118

IV The Cycle of Kings and Queens

About This Time...	123
A Wolf Story	126
The Crop Haired Girl	129
The Woman in the Castle	132
Grace and Elizabeth	135
The Seven Sisters	138
Padraig and the Púca	141
The Witch of Kilkenny	144

The Hags with the Bags	147
The Spit Milk	150
Bear Witness	153
The Woman of the House	157
An Bean Feasa	162
Her and Her Bottle	166
The Death Cry	169
Reflections	173
A Harvest Tale	176
For Ireland	180
About the Author	184
Also by Lora O'Brien	186

Foreword

What The Experts Are Saying About This Book

To be honest, I'd always found reading the old legends and stories of the Celtic lands rather daunting and difficult. I just couldn't relate to them. Lora O'Brien's new work gives useful guidance in this respect, when she says:

"If you're new to all this, or just not very familiar with the Irish source material, don't worry about it. Just enjoy the stories and you'll be learning and connecting more than you realise."

And this mixture of the re-telling of ancient legend and historical record enabled me to do just that. The stories are readable and flow well. They are full of magical themes such as ritual and power, animals and shape-shifting. But above all there is the landscape in which these tales are acted out, not only as a background but as an essential feature of the action.

The stories are short but always hinted at the possibility of more that could be told. We may perhaps look forward to more in the same vein.

Oh, and I enjoyed reading them very much!

Philip Heselton, author of 'Gerald Gardner and the Cauldron of Inspiration', and 'Doreen Valiente: Witch'.

Lora O'Brien has a dry sense of humour and quick wit that make her writing a genuine pleasure to experience. In 'Tales of Old Ireland Retold' the reader sees the benefit of this combination, getting a taste of Irish mythology and folklore through masterful modern re-tellings that capture the spirit of the originals with a fresh voice. Covering everything from the arrival of the Tuatha Dé Danann in Ireland to stories of púca and leannán sí, this book should be essential reading for anyone interested in Irish mythology or Irish folklore who wants to have both the knowledge and the heart of the stories.

Morgan Daimler, author of 'Gods and Goddesses of Ireland', and 'A New Dictionary of Fairies'.

When we read the myths and tales as they come down to us from the early Irish manuscripts, they can seem to belong to another time, like creatures frozen in amber. A wealth of detail is there, but fixed in archaic language, cryptic and obscured by the layers of time. Lora's tales breathe new life into these treasured myths, as if someone resurrected the creature in the amber and set it in vibrant motion before us. They read like the lucid memories of one who was there to see, sharing the recollections of a long life over a shared drink. These stories are the voice of Ireland, composed and articulated through the witty, insightful, and unflinching prose of someone who walks the land every day drinking from its deep well of memory.

- Morpheus Ravenna, author of 'The Book of The Great Queen: The Many Faces of the Morrigan from Ancient Legends to Modern Devotions'.

Preface

In 2012, I began writing Irish stories.

So enchanted with the Tales of Old Ireland was I, so utterly taken with the magic and mystery of them - from ancient myth to recent folklore - and so afraid that they were being lost, forgotten, resigned to a dry and dusty history, deemed irrelevant... that I started to retell them.

Some were published in magazines, some on my own website. Some were written spontaneously, simply to delight and honour my friends.

In 2016, I began to get serious about Irish stories.

I started to publish one per month, exclusively for Patrons supporting me at the $3 per month reward level, on my Patreon profile.

[You can sign up as a Patron yourself if you'd like to receive a new Irish tale directly every month, so you don't have to wait a few years for the next collection... https://Patreon.com/LoraOBrien]

Now, in 2018, my first collection of our Tales of Old Ireland is available.

I can only hope they bring you as much joy and hope in the reading of them, as they have brought me in the writing of them.

See you in the next book,
   Slán Go Fóill!

I

The Mythological Cycle

1

About This Time...

The Mythological Cycle is a set of tales about different tribes and races said to have arrived in Ireland in 5 great waves, before the coming of the Gaels... but the bulk of it tells the stories of the Tuatha Dé Danann, often translated as the tribe or people of Danú, or Anú.

The term gained popularity when used by Arbois de Jubainville (c. 1881–1883), and can be seen to describe the native (pre-christian) spiritual beliefs, stories and even practice of Ireland.

With the arrival of the Milesians we see the beginning of the Gaelic culture in Ireland, and an end to the Mythological cycle. The Milesians were supposed to have come from Iberia (Spain and Portugal), but whether that's true or not is anybody's guess, and a hotly debated topic in Irish academia, insofar as the scholars really get hot under the collar at all. They're a staid bunch, for the most part. So, luke-warmly debated might be a better description really.

Gaelic language and culture pretty certainly began in earlier pagan times, stretching through to Christian occupation and on into the Late Medieval era. I think it's neat and tidy to link it with the Iron Age, but I'm open to those tepid debates and learning more on the topic. We'd be talking roughly 500 BCE (Before Common Era) for the start of that period, and it continued to about 400 CE (Common Era), with the gradual takeover of the new religion moving into the Early Medieval time frame, and being well enough established by 600 CE.

If I was pushed for a date so, a setting for the Mythological period, I'd say we have stories in there stretching back to our earliest times, in one form or another, for humans have walked this land for at least 12,500 years according to latest evidence (Alice and Gwendoline Cave, County Clare). So this cycle of tales could possibly run through Paleolithic, Mesolithic (Hunter Gatherers - 10,000 years ago), Neolithic (New Stone Age, earliest Farmers - 6,500 years ago), into the Copper and Bronze Ages (earliest Metalworkers - 4,500 years ago), and ending with the coming of the Iron Age (newer, harder metals - 2,500 years ago).

Of course we don't know exactly when these stories were first being spoken, as the versions that remain to us were not recorded until much, much later, and incompletely at that.

But we do know that the Beings and themes they tell of will speak to us of an ancient time, every time we hear them told.

And that's good enough for me.

2

The Guardians

They met in the middle.

In the glen, by the smoke of a wet wood fire, they came together. Under the dark of their moon, the stars of their sky stretching over, they met in the middle.

From Falias came Mórfessa, dark and cold as the earth stone, bringing the depth of knowledge and understanding. In her pocket she carried the wisdom of ages, and in the middle she placed the Lia Fáil – stone of sovereignty.

From Goirias came Esras, hot and bright as the fever's burn, walking with dutiful care and affection. In her pocket she carried the fire of eventual comfort, and in the middle she placed the Sword of the King – unconquerable once blooded.

From Findias came Uiscias, fluid and fresh as the river's passing, flowing across the land with purpose and patience. In her pocket she carried the fast flow of justice, and in the middle she placed the Spear of Light – piercing with victory.

From Murias came Semias, stout and guarded as the sea fortress, moving carefully and deliberately to where she was needed. In her pocket she carried the rivet that held all together, and in the middle she placed the Cauldron of the Chief – giving of plenty to all.

Guardians gathered, gifts given. They met in the middle.

Esras spoke first. Of the sickness which plagued the people, with scorching intensity of the blistering seeping infections, the fervid fear stalking her once warm city, and of their loving duty to act in the interests of the tribe. The difficult decision was called for - a slashing burn to destroy, followed by the new growth, guided and fed from the cleansed and cared for remains of the old.

Uiscias spoke next. Of the turgid waters swollen with death and disease, with a well of sadness of the pale poisoned beauty of once fair streams, and of the wisdom needed to act in the interests of the tribe. The difficult decision was called for – a shaft of fatty lard to clog and grease the life giving waters beyond sustenance, followed by the inevitable flood of departure.

Semias spoke then. Of the storm lashing and breaking of ramparts, with rot and decay untended and unwatched in the once walled fortresses, and of the doughty necessity to act in the interests of the tribe. The difficult decision was called for – an emptying of the land and salting the earth, gathering and rationing hitherto plentiful provisions, in preparation for the journey ahead.

And then spoke Mórfessa.

Of the scattering of learning, with shallow thinking and easy speech too common, insincerity and dishonesty veining her once honourable foundations, and of the sovereign knowledge needed to regroup and bed down in the interests of the tribe. The difficult decision was called for – releasing the sovereign stones which held safety in this land, and seeking to refortify in another, to find and build boundaries in a new space, for depth of study and rightful rule.

They met in the middle, and so the decision was made.

And the best of their tribe was gathered under Danú, the mother. In the four cities – Goirias, Findias, Murias and Failias – they acquired knowledge and science and magic with which to mark the way.

From Goirias they brought the sword of Nuada, and no man would escape from it by reason of its venom, and when it was drawn from its battle-scabbard there was no resisting it.

From Findias was brought the spear which Lugh had, battle would never go against him who had it in hand.

From Muirias was brought the cauldron of the Dagda, and no company would go from it unsatisfied.

Then, from Failias was brought the Lia Fáil, the sovereign stone ever watched for by the Great Queen Mór Ríoghain, and it would not utter a cry but under every king or queen that should take Ireland. From it the new land would be named, the fortified island that is Inis Fáil.

The four sages in those cities – Esrus, Uiscias, Semias and Mórfessa – these were the four poets, the guardians and guides, with whom the Tuatha De Danann acquired wisdom and knowledge. For this was said, and carried, and written and told.

But when the tribe travelled to Inis Fáil, the four great guardians remained. Under the dark of their moon, the stars of their sky stretching over, they watched the ships of the tribe leave their land. That was the last of their stories that would be told, and they knew it, and they stayed.

Now, that's not the last tales we'll hear told of the tribe of Danú though, the Tuatha Dé Danann... but they're all stories for another day.

3

Black Birds

Eochaidh walked.

The grass was cool and soft beneath his bare feet, lush with the promise of new summer's growth. He knew himself to be walking through fields behind the house of his father, Erc, and that it was Bealtaine, for the smell of the smoke of their fires was on the air, lingering from the night before when the driving of beasts between flame had added the tinge of singed hair and hide to the heady wood smoke scent piling into the sky.

Stopping to breathe it deeply, he closed his eyes to the sound of trees rustling on the boundary of his father's fields, and felt the gathering warmth of the sun caress his face and neck, while his feet drew damp and cool dew from the grass. Opening his eyes, he looked at how the light sparkled through this collecting water, tiny fire gem points dotting through rolling green pasture.

It made his feet cold from below, despite the heat on his head and neck from above – though he wondered, briefly, what had happened to his shoes. Trees rustled again, leaves and boughs slipping and scraping a little off each other in the gathering breeze.

With that wind came a new smell.

Rolling in across the open ground came a musty, ripe odour that crept into his nostrils like something living, trying to make its crawling way inside his head. Each gust brought a new waft, an aroma he couldn't quite place – so out of place with all he knew here. And the smell of... salt on the air, mingling with the soft reek of old, decaying things.

The squall roughened around him, his clothing now moving with the twisting airstreams flowing over the land, harrying the longer grasses and causing chaos in the branches of the trees. He watched them bend and snap together, sensing from behind him the approach of the source of that odour so alien to him, even as the sky began to darken overhead.

He didn't want to see it, whatever was coming, though he could feel its approach gathering strength and power, just as he knew the people of his father's land were rising against what came. He saw them appear on the horizon, a mass of running shouting bodies entering the field, as if towards a vigorous battle, with shouts and raised weapons, their shining spears and swords pointing to the sky.

Yet it gave him no comfort, knowing these brave folk gathered, for he could smell them and hear the storm from behind him, then the raucous calls of the great, black, birds he now saw with his eyes as the air blackened around him and he dropped to the grass to escape their mass against the sky.

The cold of his bare feet spread quickly without the warming comfort of the sun on his skin, as the birds flew overhead in a seemingly endless stream of dark feathers and noise. His people fought them bravely, but ahead all was confusion, destruction... until the cold earth became the chill of a grave, the dark depth of a hollow hill, and he understood he would never feel warmth again in this life.

A brief respite, as one of his father's folk raised from the fray, rushing towards the noblest of the birds as he could see it, and struck off one of its wings, so the iron tang of its blood reeked through them, clearing a path back towards him as they veered and swerved to avoid the bright red among the black clouding his vision, and the stink of old iron from a forest floor wound its way through his brain...

Eochaidh woke.

Complete darkness still surrounded him, but it was the enclosing safety of the rath walls, a little stale, and due the fresh earth coating after a long winter – that would be one of the first jobs of the summer. The cold remained, seeped deep in his bones from the clammy dream sweat covering his skin and his bare feet, having kicked off the bed covering in his dream thrashing, fighting off... birds?

Yes, a great flock of black birds, coming from the depths of the Ocean. They settled over all of the land, and fought with the people of Ireland. They brought confusion, and destroyed his people, though one of them had struck the noblest of the birds and cut off one of its wings.

Tomorrow, he would ask the druid Cesard what it might mean.

Tonight though, this Monday of the first week in May, he would return to sleep, for the work was all around him now the Bealtaine feasting was done. And so he did, that night, return to his slumber.

But he could not quite shake the memory of the tang of iron on the air.

That's not the first or the last time that someone got a portent of things to come, on the island of Ireland, by no means is it!

But sure, they are all stories for another day.

4

The True Tale of Tailtiu

She watched them come.

Nervous now, on the day of beginning, a fortnight before Lughnasadh, for the Aonach Tailteann. Nervous for the work that awaited her, as she would tell the tale of Tailtiu. This year was the first she was ready.

On the north bank of the river of black water did they gather, coming from every side of the island, and from over the sea even – the cousins from Alba would venture the waves to make it home too, for the fair. People already garnered the marriage hollow with early blooms, though the main flowers would come with August and the turning to harvest time.

She knew the stables over at Cnoc Aidi were already filled with the horses they'd brought, ready to run the races from there and finish at the heart of the fair. All the preparations were in place for the funerary games held in honour of the goddess, and there would be hurling, athletic, gymnastic and equestrian clashes of all kinds, with running, long-jumping, high-jumping, throwing, spear-casting, sword and shield contests, wrestling, boxing, handball, swimming, of course the horse-racing, chariot-racing, spear jumping, slinging competitions, bow and arrow shows, and every sort of test to display the assembled physical endurance and skill. But not just that! The games had always included the tests of mind and crafting just as evenly – so there were board games, literary, musical, oratorical, and story-telling competitions, singing and dancing contests, tested rivalries between goldsmiths, jewellers, and artificers in the precious metals, long running contests between spinners, weavers and dyers, and the makers of shields and weapons of war – with the bardic events some of the most competitive of all.

And here was she, in all her unproven youth, being given the responsibility of telling the tale of Tailtiu, in whose honour the Aonach had been started and always held!

Knowing she needed to stop watching, and take a walk to soothe her stresses, she went where her legs would carry her. Down by the river, and along its banks a while, 'til she had followed it round the first sharp curve, and the festival preparations were long out of sight. Walking on, she had passed about three forrachs a-pace, and the river's black curves and flow had her calmed and centred. She realised then she had come to the old barrow mound on the bend, and decided resting there would be just the grandest, until she was right to return and get settled in to the fair.

The sun was high about the hill as she climbed the slight incline and settled on the gentle slope. She closed her eyes and warmed her bones well, and in her idle thought, she hoped the sun's strength could beam down through the soil to warm the bones of the ancestor buried below, for that was the purpose of a barrow – to mark the grave of one who was important.

"Go raibh maith agat, mo chara."

Starting at the sound of a voice so close, she opened her eyes to see a woman seated by her side, who had thanked her so and called her friend.

Ah, but it wasn't the first time she'd met one such as this face to face, so to speak, for isn't it well known that the bardic ways are close to the

Other World, and that they open an easy gate to that life beyond?

So, she spoke to the woman, and knew her for who she was – the very Tailtiu, foster mother of Lugh and Queen of the Firbolg, whose tale she would come to tell. Never one to miss an opportunity, she asked for the story from source, then and there, and this is what she got to bring back to the Aonach Fair...

"I came hither leading the Fir Bolg host to Caill Chuan, after the high battle with the newcomers to this land. Caill Chuan, it was a thicket of trees from Escir to Ath Drommann, from the Great Bog, a long journey, from the Sele to Ard Assuide. Commur, Currech, Crích Linde, Ard Manai where the spears used to be; the hounds of Cairpre killed their quarry on the land of Tipra Mungairde.

Great that deed that was done with the axe's help by me, the reclaiming of meadowland from the even wood by the daughter of my father, gentle Magmor.

When the fair wood was cut down by me, roots and all, out of the ground, before the year's end it became Bregmag, it became a plain blossoming with clover. But it was great work, and not wholesome, truly, is it to have a face glowing like the coal at the end of your work, for the sake of woods or pride of timber.

My heart burst in my body from the strain beneath my royal vest; and long was the sorrow, long the weariness as I lay in sickness after heavy toil; the men of the island of Erin to whom I was in bondage after that war, they came to receive my last behest.

Feeble I was but not speechless, and I told them in my weakness that they should hold funeral games to lament me, and that I would be buried in royal state, with impressive druidical rites, and about this time I died, leaving behind the gift of the chief Fair of noble Erin. A fair with gold, with silver, with games, with music of chariots, with adornment of body and of soul by means of knowledge and eloquence. A fair without wounding or robbing of any man, without trouble, without dispute, without reaving, without challenge of property, without suing, without law-sessions, without evasion, without arrest.

A fair without sin, without fraud, without reproach, without insult, without contention, without seizure, without theft, without redemption: unbroken truce of the fair the while through Erin and Alba alike, while folk went in and came out without any rude hostility. And this finest fair has been held by the fairy host, a fair every single year, by the Fir Bolg, who were there, by the Tuatha De Danann, and by the Children of Mil thereafter."

And the white-sided Tailtiu left her then, and uttered in her land again the true prophecy; that so long as every prince should accept her, the land of Erin should not be without perfect song.

Now, that's not the only time a bard, druid, or poet ever got a great old tale from beyond the grave... but sure, they're all stories for another day.

5

The Union at the River

She arrives early, as is her wont, to prepare the place, and prepare herself, for their meeting.

Both so busy, so much to do, travelling the land, the sea, the sky. Guiding and guarding the island, her people. She sighs, just a little. So much to do.

But not this day. This day is their Samhain meeting, always each year, and she will put the work aside and take pleasure in the preparation, in the waiting for his arrival. Nine plaited tresses hang heavy down her back, and she takes each, one by one, and releases the magic that she tied within. She will reform them later, as she does every year, to secure the spells once more. Long red hair now sits in nine smooth waves across her fair shoulders, as she steps from the ruddy cloak, its deep scarlet folds discarded on the bank of the River Unshin.

Her first naked foot she places carefully by Echumech, the water to the South. Straddling the clear flow that runs the middle boundary, the other bare foot she sets by Loscoindoib, the water to the North. Such simple joy to bend into that pure stream, to feel it's icy kiss on her flesh, to dip and scoop and splash the cleansing liquid to her sacred centre, with thigh muscles flexing to keep her spread and open position balanced and sure.

An awareness first. She senses him draw near, their constant connection pulsing stronger as distance closes. Then a noise, a small rustle in the undergrowth surrounding the Glen. Slight, subtle, and she deliberately pays him no attention upon his approach, though a small smile touches her lips. Continuing her ablutions, hands slowly rise and fall from the water, the fire of sunset light sparking through each moving droplet, each glistening pearl of water that settles on skin. She can see him now from the corner of her eye, still and sheltered by the trees. She knows he likes to watch her, drink in her face, her form, after so long apart, and so she sets a steady pace to the ritual, while he remains away, light dappling across his large body, standing with his massive club in hand and waiting, savouring, until his inevitable approach is signalled.

When she is finished, and not a moment before, she raises her head and meets his eye with a glint to match his, her smile beckoning him closer now the time is upon them. An answering grin lighting his face, he steps from cover and is over to her in three long strides. Showing no difficulty, he reaches across the river and lifts her into his arms, her head coming to rest in comfort on his broad shoulder while his lips find her ear and begin to speak the words that are kept just for her. With a delicacy and gentleness that is still surprising to her from one so big, he lays her down on the bank and lies beside, still speaking softly such private sounds as are shared between couples. His questions she answers, his queries are reassured, their marriage vows renewed and refreshed as they unite once more in power and strength, in love and tenderness, in pleasure and joy.

Afterwards, lying sated and secure together in the bed of the married couple, the Mórrígan gives her mate, Dagda, such advice as any sensible Queen would impart to her King before a battle. To clear the land of support which would prove useful to the enemy. To gather the Aes Dana, the Tuatha, their tribe, to this place together for safety and council. She promises him her aid, of course she will fight for their tribe, their people, with magic and with blood. She decides to attack the enemy king directly, the Fomorian Indech Mac De Domnann. She will take from his body the blood of his heart and his very kidneys, denying him valour and battle-ardour. Then she will return to the tribe bearing two fists of blood, to prophecy the utter destruction of their foes.

There is much more to be told of the battle that followed, fought across Magh Tuireadh... but they are all stories for another day.

6

The Brush and Comb

She had left it too long again.

Out in the war. Doing the work in this world. Carrying the weight of it.

Too long here, and too far from home now. Not enough left to get her back to her world. Damn it, she would have to go to him.

She began to walk there. Oh she knew the ways well enough, and had been there enough times by choice, by design, by right. In different circumstances, with a different outlook, a different intent, a visit there was almost... welcome. A bright interlude, if brief, that would entertain and often even refresh her for the work out there. He knew well how to host, after all. And the food was always good.

It wasn't too far to there from here, by the ways of this world – as the crow flies, one might say – but the weight of it all had made her so heavy. With doing her work she took it all on, took it all inside herself, to shape and twist and mould and bend and form again into what should be. But sometimes, at these times, she took too much, and with all she already did, there wasn't enough inside in herself to change it and make it right the way it could be, and she became so heavy with it all. It stuck her here, in this world that wasn't hers.

Her feet fell flat on the earth with each step. There was nothing left to lift her, to let her dance and turn. Her arms hung at her sides, her head drooped down, her shoulders fell forward as she walked. It wasn't too far now, she could make it that far at least, even if no further, and then he would be there, and this would be... better. He had made it better before, the once or twice she had left it too long and not been close enough to get to home. He was good that way, though she was never sure what he'd done, exactly. His ways were yet a mystery to her, although she saw so much in every other direction, there was much about him she did not see, and could not read if she did.

It vexed her.

Thoughts on her destination only now, on having enough, just enough, to get her there. One step. One step. One step. Not seeing further than the next step – perhaps the clearest indication of all just how close she had come to the end of herself.

When the rain began, it covered her quickly and soaked her through, adding directly to the weight of all she carried, of all she had become. The wool of her cloak did not keep it from her flesh, becoming sodden and adding so much burden to her shoulders that she released the pins and dropped it behind her, allowing the ice of the downpour to seep through her skin and down to the bones of her, draining her even more.

The brú was in sight when her strength finally ran out. In truth, it had run out long before that, and only her will had driven her on. But it was with the light and the hearth smoke and the noise of his place in view on the horizon that her feet stopped stepping, and the weight she carried deep in the core of her finally felled her to the earth of this world.

...

She woke to darkness.

The round walls of a chamber surrounded her, interlocking stone and the fresh dug scent of cool earth. A new build, and she knew his handiwork well enough by now. So, he had found her when she fell. He had lain her on a palette of woven ivy. A favourite of hers in this world, and he'd remembered well. There was a passage beyond, leading from the chamber, with light enough coming through to make out a three legged stool by the side of her bed, and around it on the ground were... wood shavings? Her mind filled in the blanks, and she could see where he'd sat by her side, and carved as he waited – an old habit of his in troubled times, to find the heart of the wood and release its true form. And on the stool, the shape of a thing. She reached out her hand and picked it up, feeling with her thumb the smooth rounded edge on one side, and the fine wide teeth on the other. Touching her hair, she felt how it had been released from its braids, and combed out smooth.

Well. Time enough to re-tie those responsibilities when she went back out into the worlds.

Rising, and naked enough to raise her own eyebrow, she stepped towards the passage, moving silently on the balls of her feet. It was a short connecting path to another chamber, the same size as the first, but seeming so much smaller for being filled with his large frame, and a crackling fire besides. She stayed in the shadows, completely quiet and well hidden, and watched – his form, the movement of his hands - as he turned carefully in the small space, feeding the fire from a stock of wood by the wall behind him, and settled back again to more carving. His knife blade glinted liquid fire back to her, and bounced it off the chamber roof, where a small opening released the smoke to the sky.

"So you're awake lass? I wasn't sure you'd make it back from that one. You've been gone... a while."

She never could hide from him, not completely.

"What's that you carve?" She didn't want to discuss what had brought her here, nor how close she had come again this time. He knew it, and she knew it. And they both knew she'd do it again if she had to. It was just the way of things, and the work that had to be done.

His frown lifted a little, and though there was no softness or smile to his voice – he never did move from concern to contentment quickly at all, for he felt it too deeply – she heard the care for her there as he said, "It's the back of a brush, to match your comb. Your hair was in an awful mess, and I thought..."

Deep brown eyes sought hers, and she was sorry for the fear she saw they held, and the pain. They both knew there was nothing they could do for it – she had her work, as he had his – but she didn't like to see it nonetheless. Circling round the fire, she stood behind him, causing a hiss and indrawn breath as her cold hand found his broad shoulder, but the usual warmth of his flesh soon balanced him out. He relaxed back to lean against her, heaving a sigh as his head leaned to her thigh, and the fingers of her other hand played idly with his curls while she delayed the inevitable for just a few moments longer.

"I'll walk you out lass. I know you've to be on your way. I'm... I'm glad you came."

...

A little way beyond the brú, where they'd walked together in the silence of those who can't speak as they'd like, she stopped. She could feel the worlds calling again, the endless ebb and flow, the push and pull, the patterns forming and unforming. It was past time to take back up with her work.

Turning to tell him goodbye, for now, she caught sight of the two chambers he had built for her rest above on the brow of the hill by the brú.

And now it was her turn to frown.

"Can you tell me, good husband, why exactly yon mounds are shaped so perfectly like the breasts I sometimes wear upon my very chest?"

He had the grace to blush just a little at that, and told her the story of how he had found her, in the pouring rain and soaked through without a cloak, on that very spot – and hadn't her lovely form been outlined against the sky so perfectly that, well, he couldn't help but notice the shape she wore. It wasn't a decision he'd made at the time, though he did observe it himself afterwards indeed... but maybe he had been influenced by her particular shape at that time, and sure was that a bad thing at all now, really, in the grand scheme of things?!

The glint in his eye as he looked at her a little shame-faced caused a laugh despite herself, and she felt it lift her, to let her dance and turn.

It was a very different form that looked at him then from the branches of a tree. He wasn't sure a crow should have eyebrows, or how he felt about having one of them raised at him... but he was glad to see her form again into what should be, and glad to hear her cry on the wind in the open sky as she went back out to her work.

Turning to the brú, he went back to his... leaving the brush and comb where they were in the chambers for the next time she needed to come to him. For that was her place now.

Now, that's not the first time the Dagda and the Mórrígan came together to set things right... but sure, they are all stories for another day.

7

Lugh at Tara

It was fierce cold for sure out there, away from the light and heat of the feast. Eoghain hated gatekeeping duty, but it was his turn and that was that, so there he sat. Young Fionnuala had slipped him a wineskin full of the best from inside in the kitchens, so it wasn't as bad as it could have been at least. He could hear the occasional strain of the harp though, and the odd waft of roasted meat drifted up to him even there, causing his mouth to water and his belly to rumble, and his mood to darken even further. He'd told Fionnuala there was no need for guard duty this night – the walls at Tara were the soundest in the land, and sure everyone who would be coming was inside already. Nobody missed a feast of the Tuatha Dé Danann.

Sudden thumping from outside the gates jolted him out of a doze and made a liar of him, for there was most definitely someone there who wasn't inside already, and didn't want to miss the feast at Tara, judging by the clatter they were causing. Eoghain made his way down to the small gate and pulled back the hatch so he could see the head of whoever was outside.

The warrior, for he was undoubtedly a warrior, was alone, and he looked pleasant enough. There was a fierce brightness about him, even in the gloom of the evening, which Eoghain couldn't account for, so he left that thought alone and reverted to his customary gate query – who was this stranger disturbing the peace at Tara, and what did he want. He was called Lugh, this bright warrior, and he wanted to join the feast within. But sure the seats were all full, and everyone who was supposed to be coming was inside already; what did they need another for?

Well, it turns out this young man could lay claim as a master Builder, one of the best in all of Éireann, and surely that would gain him a place at the King's table? But no, Eoghain said, for the Tuatha Dé Danann already had the best of Builders, and sure what would they be needing another for? Well, it turns out this young man was also a master Brazier, one of the best in all of Éireann, and could keep the fires in all of Tara lit and tended no matter what came. Surely that would gain him a place at the King's table? But no, Eoghain said, for the Tuatha Dé Danann already had the best of Braziers, and sure what would they be needing another for? Well, it turns out this young man was also a master Harper, one of the best in all of Éireann, and his music would soothe the very soul of any who heard it. Surely that would gain him a place at the King's table? But no, Eoghain said, for the Tuatha Dé Danann already had the best of Harpers, and sure what would they be needing another for? They progressed through a range of skills: Lugh was a Smith who could craft with any metal, a Champion of all games and arts, a Poet who could charm or curse with equal skill, an Historian who would recite the families and battles of all Éireann through the ages, a Cup-bearer who would never spill a drop, a Magician who could control the very world around them, and even a Physician who could cure all ills, excepting if a head be cut clean off. But no, Eoghain said, for the Tuatha Dé Danann had all of these people skilled in such things, and sure what would they be needing another for?

Ah now, says Lugh, and tell me Gatekeeper – but do you have any man or woman within the walls of Tara who can do ALL of these things?

Eoghain was forced to admit that no, they did not, and the stranger was welcomed on the back of that. Lugh was announced as the Ildánach – the many skilled one – and that was the first we heard of him, though not the last. But sure, they are all stories for another day.

8

The Harper

Clochend stood by the gateway as the first strains of harp music filtered through to them.

"So, he has come."

"As you knew he would, daughter", said the Bodb. "We foresaw this many cycles back, and now he is here."

They listened as the music grew, seeming louder than one person could accomplish on one harp, filling the chamber in which they stood with the – not unpleasant, granted – sounds of his playing.

"Is it two harps he's playing on though?"

"So it sounds", she replied. "Skillful, at least. I'll not go to him though, as I said."

"No matter to me." The Bodb shrugged. "He can get no closer. The guardians will see to that, and they will stay as long as is needed."

Outside the Sidhe of Femhen, Cliach played his two harps. He had first tried to enter, planning to claim the wolf-head warrior woman Clochend as his own, but the Bodb who ruled here must have already divined the design he had placed on the daughter of this Munster Sidhe, even while Cliach sat above in his own Sidhe Báine in Connacht hatching his plans of wooing, and solicitation.

For he'd heard tell often of the woman's might, and it brought a great grief to him, urging him to take it, to keep it for his own. At home there were wolves aplenty that required management and control, and if Cliach could take that power he would soon rise through the ranks of his own Sidhe. His king, Smirdubh Mac Smáil of the three Rosses atop the mountain, valued greatly the family of the Bodb, and would be fierce content to have one of the daughters in his tuath.

But when Cliach arrived here to the Sidhe on this mountain, he was met with a boundary and guardians to greet him. Sent out by the Bodb, these guarding creatures were formed of fire and flame, cased in stone hide, scalding the land with each step. Alive but not living. They formed that boundary over which he could not cross, so he had sat outside the circle, and began to play. His harps contained the magic of his Sidhe, and they were a balanced pair. As long as he played them together, he needed no food or drink, no sleep or rest, and no weather could touch him. If he could not enter the keep to claim his prize, he would entice her out beyond the boundaries... and take her then.

And so he played the charms of his noble chant, over and over, through morning and night. Many travelled to hear his harp, sweet sounding as it resonated through the mountain. Throngs of chiefs admired the music that he made. A host of the Sidhe gathered, curious as to the outcome, this challenge to the magic of the Bodb – and they stayed on site, with plenty of delights, until the tuatha of the Sidhe of Femhen were plagued with indolent fairies, bent on endless durance to the final outcome. Whatever that might be.

So passed a full cycle of seasons, a year as we call it.

Still Cliach played.

"I wish to end this. Enough is enough, and he will not stop of his own accord with such an audience, for his pride is at stake now."

"No matter to me." The Bodb shrugged. "Your wish and your will, daughter, is what matters here."

"I will go to ground, and take the shape of the earth. I will go to him then, and he shall have a woman's might indeed."

At the boundary, the guardians ceased their scalding steps.

The first rumbles were felt by the gathered host, and it rippled unease among them, so they began to move away. The harper started to tremble in dawning horror at what could shake the very earth such as this. Unmoving, the guardians watched the first cracks appear in the ground by their feet, splitting with hisses of steam escaping, as fire rose from the heart of the world to spill downhill across the grass. Still Cliach played sweet melody on his two harps, 'til the earth beneath him burst, and Crochend broke forth in full fire form. Seizing him even as he died of terror, she took the harper, and his harps, down to where she dwelled, followed by the guardians – their work complete - while water began to flow into the hole she had made in the earth. This formed what men later called Loch Bel Dracon, 'the Lake of the Dragon's Mouth', atop the mountain.

Then all was silent at the Sidhe of Femhen.

9

The Children of my Sister

Never had two sisters been closer.

Oh, that's not the way the tale is told now of course. Nowadays it's all about the wicked step-mother, and the sweet, sacrificed lambs. Or swans, as it were.

Now they say I was jealous of Aoibh; that I'm a prideful, awful woman who despised her sister's children and the love they shared with their adoring father. So they say! Do they ever tell the real reason I despised those scheming little gullet slitters? Why I wanted them dead? Well, let me tell you why.

Myself and my sister were each others' world. We were never apart, from morning 'til night. When our father, Bodb Dearg, became king of the Tuatha Dé Danann, his clansman Lear was fit to be tied. Like, spitting fire so he was, he thought it'd be him chosen for sure. Lear was a strong man, with a good following, and our father didn't want to make an enemy of him. It might've been either of us chosen, for we were both as lovely as any in the land, but in the end it was Aoibh he handed over for marriage to Lear, and she went with good grace but no joy in her heart.

It wasn't a terrible union, after a while, sure she grew to love him and

I even got fair fond of him after years of regular visits. Four children she bore him, and from the very start I could smell the badness off them. She wouldn't listen of course, she'd not hear a word said against them, but there were times I caught her watching their antics with a fierce worried look on her face. As for Lear, he'd chop his own ears off rather than hear my concerns, or more likely, my lips for daring to speak them. He adored the very ground they tread on, and after the first attempt I shut up fast.

But I could see it growing in them every day. The eldest one, Fionnuala, was the pack leader. The twins Fiacre and Conn had followed soon after her, and they continued to follow whatever dance she led them on. By the time the youngest, Aodh, arrived to complete the set, they had all the servants terrified of their spiteful tricks, and the impunity in which they could work.

The last time I was in their keep as a visitor, there was a kitchen cat and her kittens out the back parlour, and the cooks looking after them well. The mother was a fine ratter, and a valuable asset to any household. One of the days I was passing through, the cooks were in a tizzy, as every single kitten had disappeared, all six of them, and their mother was wailing and making a fuss such as they'd never heard. She just paced back and forth in the parlour, refusing to leave the household, calling and howling for her kits. And nobody knew what had happened to them.

I knew, I knew those harrowing butchers had made off with those poor kittens. I went to Aoibh, and told her my suspicions, and she confessed she had seen the youngest, Aodh, carrying them away the previous day. When all four children denied any knowledge, all the while sharing smug looks and snickers, it broke a dam inside her, her worst fears realised, and we went together to Lear to confront him on the matter, and make sure they were taken in hand.

Fionnuala had gotten to him first. She spun a tale of wicked women plotting against his innocent babes, and he fell for every word. He twisted it further to make sure I took the brunt of blame, and I was out on my ear with a ban on any return before I could barely blink.

Seven years I was kept away, until the day I was called to my father's hall for news of my sister's death, in circumstances I knew were the work of a mortal hand, though made to look accidental. And the further blow - that I was to take her place, to be sent off as step-mother to the children I was sure had murdered my beloved sister.

That's not the last that was ever heard of the children of Lear... but sure, they are all stories for another day.

10

The Crooked Bloody God

He looked at her, his Druid wife, and said again, "Are ya sure?"

"I'm sure as sure can be", says she, and turns to carry on.

And behind her, they all carried on. Some were still walking, and upright, for the most part. Some stumbled, and fell, and picked themselves up, or were picked up to carry on. Some few had risen upright for the last time some time ago, but still they drew breath, so were being carried or dragged behind on makeshift sledges of branches. And some, some had fallen a ways back and would never rise again.

It was a long journey they travelled, and none of them in the sort of health to take it on. But they carried on.

From Tara they had come, the hosts of Banba. To Magh Slecht they journeyed, the Plain of Prostrations. The wife of Tighearnmas told them it must be done, for the plague that ravaged them must be slated, with sacrifice and service to the Old One.

She had warned him, her husband king so bright and shining at Tara, not to forget the Old Ways, the Old Ones, in the talk of the new god king that tainted the land. What did that one know of the folk of this island? His land was sand and dust, sun and sour breath, speaking of peace to a people who lived by battle. Priests of the new god were jealous of his worship, they left no room for the old ways which had generously moved and shifted to accommodate and include. And now the tangled root took hold; in the minds of men there was power to be had, to control and conquer with the ways of the new god king, and the male priests who served him.

She had warned him, and he had not listened. And now the tribes fell to the poison that grew in their very hearts. Waves of plague washed the island, and where was the new god king in that? The silent péist at the heart of the apple is all, sitting and consuming, while its very presence spoiled the fruit and bounty around it.

Samhain approached, and she had stood and watched as his people, her people, rotted and fell. This, then, was the result of ignorance, of not offering the Wizened One his due – he must take it on himself. She had offered the bull at Lughnasadh, had overseen the priestess of Áine become warrior and consort as was right... but too few had paid heed, that year or those gone before. Too few had stepped forward to run with the boar, to risk the blood and gore, to sacrifice and give due to he who lies beneath the land and drinks the blood that falls or flows to him.

So, she had resolved to travel the mists herself as the year turned, to use the time between times to make some recompense. At last her king had listened, as his people dropped poisoned around him. And now, now they journeyed to the Plain of the Old Ones. Through many mists they journeyed, and at the rise above, the shroud began to clear, enough to make out the stones that stood below.

She had timed it well. The sun was setting beyond the Plain, lifting the silvered glints threaded through twelve stones, ranged in ranks while the thirteenth stood proud, blazing golden in the dying light. The people sighed, some buried belief of souls gaining succour from the ancient sight, the wisdom of bones and blood that sang now for being in the right place, at the right time. They carried on.

Down to the Plain of Prostration they went, stirring the Old Ones; they beat palms, they bruised bodies, wailing now to the Crooked Bloody God, they shed showers of tears, weeping prostrate for the evil they had wrought upon themselves. Round Cromm Cruach there the hosts did obeisance, so that the tops of their foreheads and the gristle of their noses and the caps of their knees and the ends of their elbows broke – and three fourths of the people of Éire perished at those prostrations, through that long dark night. But with the dawn of the new morning, some of them stood. And they carried on.

There was much and much more, evil and ill being brought to the island beyond that time, by the new god and his priests... but sure, they are all stories for another day.

11

The Sorcerous Sisters

"Be Neit, I call you. Woman of Battle, Bringer of Madness."

Nemhain stood forth, while her sister dipped fingers into the thick red paste and drew the whorls and swirls on skin already flushed dark with excitement, with blood rushing beneath. Eyes, lips, cheeks anointed. Forehead, nose, chin anointed. Patterns and symbols of old, as their mother wore before battle, as her mother, her mother's mother, and all through their line back through time.

She felt the effects of the paste begin to seep through her skin – limbs strengthened and muscles defined, tendons tightened, ready to spring and dance. War Dancer, she was called, Bride of Battle. Her weapons were spear and blade, but more than that, the Voice of Fury she bore and utilised, that place where terror truly lay.

"Badbh, I call you. Fea of my heart, child of my father. Woman of Battle, Badbh Catha."

Nemhain now dipped her fingers deep into the matching black paste, rubbing it with her fingertips, enjoying the viscous sensation on her flesh as she repeated the familiar patterns and symbols on her sister's skin.

A chanting began, low and rhythmic with the drums from beyond. The sisters circled the fire, beginning their twisted dance together. Reaching to the pouches hung at each waist, they pulled forth herbs they knew by touch, their scent intensifying on contact with the air, and more so again as they threw them to the central cauldron sitting over flames. Handfuls of herbs, added and stirred, as the sisters twisted their sorcery round the circle.

Poetry she brought to bear, to add to the poisonous mix. Red-mouthed Badbh opened wide to pour forth the chanting wail, while Nemhain plumbed the wisdom of her bloodline to find the words to wreck and rhyme the enemy to where her voice could catch their ears. The fire heated those words, mixed with herbs, as the Brides of Battle ululated, undulating around the cauldron to fix their sorcerous intent.

Out into the evening they danced, once the spell was set. The daughters of Elcmar wended their way over the crest of the high boundary, then down the scrub of hillside, cauldron carried between them, carefully slipping through the landscape bearing their poisoned load into the cool dusk of the countryside. Into the water source they tipped the laced liquid, to trickle and flow down to the army encamped over the brow of the hill. Then they made their way to the cave close by, climbing into the earth to wait for full dark, and the poison to do its foul work.

Emerging to the beginning sounds of screams, the sisters smiled at each other, teeth glowing pale in blood red and shadowed faces. The intoxicated army below would be seeing shades, and monsters at every turn. The sisters slipped again to the hill crest to view the scene spread out below... the army there were scattering about, falling in their armour and on the points of their spears and sword-edges, so a hundred warriors of them died in the midst of the encampment as the sisters stood. Chaos abounded, with no man knowing friend and fearing only foe, and in that time of terror the first cry carried from on high, as Badbh opened her red mouth wide, and Nemhain unleashed the power of her

Voice upon the men below.

Such a sound had never been heard by any there, not from the first squalls of an infant on to the death throes of an elder. Such a sound had never been heard from human throat or animal gullet, not before nor since. Such a sound as she made brought panic, sheer unadulterated terror to those who heard it, those men already blinded by poison and addled by sorcery. Such a sound caused scores of men to fall immediately on their own swords, or lash out in their frenzy to kill their comrades where they stood or sat in their own fear-pissed britches, weeping as they died.

Nemhain's cries echoed the intoxication of insanity, reverberating across the landscape under the sky, while red-mouthed Badbh roared laughter and encouragement to drive it forth.

That was not the first or the last time that those sisters sang their way through the wars of men... but, they are all stories for another day.

12

The Wheel

Choice Tlachtga, they called me, when I was young, and joked each other about whether my bosom was chill as my heart within. I cared not, for I had work to do. Always more work.

My father, a giant of a man, was a master of Ireland's magic - Mug Roith he was named for the fosterage with Roth, and it tickled him greatly to remain as 'Roth's Chosen Slave', for his magic was of service and his work was with the people.

To my brother Corb he gifted the noble chant, to make use of that voice that was from the Otherworld, it seemed, and when he sang this song it brought great luck to all the people. My mother though, she had other ideas. She wanted for me the power she had, and more, for she was strong and fierce and fell, and her voice shook the trees like the wind in a storm. Derdraigen she was, and she taught me to seek strength.

I worked on the islands to the North of our isle, but I travelled far when I had a secret to seek. Sometimes I learned what I needed by wit, and charm, and sometimes by my 'choice' form. Then back to the chill lands in the North, for I had work to do. Always more work.

When the old man said he would go to seek Simon Magus, I was with him for sure. To learn the world's magic was the goal, and there was none more keen than I for that. So we travelled, away from our isle and far to the East, by land and sea to a people who were mortal in combat, in a place so strange. When we met him there, I was impressed with Simon, but more so with his sons, called Nero, Carpent, and Uetir.

They understood the work and did not think me chill, but choice, and my bosom heaved at the very sight of them, the touch of any one of their hands. From that mighty race, they were a strong bred trio, and any one of them would give me beautiful children, so I took them all to be sure of it, and quickened my own womb with three sons from them. On we worked though - the Magus, the Druid and I - and we found a way in that far off place to make a weapon, the like of which was never seen before. Mug Roith is a son of the sun, and his fascination always flickers toward the flames. My mother taught me to seek that power, and so it can hardly be surprising what we made between us.

A fire wheel we crafted fine, a burning ball that turned and scratched jagged and rough against the powders we prepared, a perfect stone that lit so bright it blinds each that sees it, that roars so loud it deafens each that hears it, that burns so red it kills all that touches of the dreadful wheel.

Now my belly grows heavy with the babes though, we travel again West, towards our home, for I won't have my sons born away from the isle. I shall name them Muach, and Cumma, and darling Doirb, and with their birth I will lay a blessing - as long as the folk of the isle hold their names in honour there will come no ruin to our home.

My time is close now, and we draw near to my land, where I will rest a while before I return to the work. There is always more work.

That's not the last we heard of Tlachtga and her rough-jagged, dreadful wheel... but they're all stories for another day.

II

The Ulster Cycle

13

About This Time...

The Ulster Cycle could - and should, some might say - be referred to as the Connacht Cycle just as easily. Of course the Boy Cú Chulainn gets all the glory, but here we see the stories of the reign of Conchobar (Conor) Mac Nessa, the King of Ulster, and Medb (Maeve), the Queen of Connacht. There is much talk of the Craebh Ruadh - the Red Branch Knights - at Emhain Macha or Navan Fort in the North, for sure. But there's also telling of the folk of Rath Crúachán or Rathcroghan in the West, and plenty more besides.

So we are likely dealing with the Iron Age in Ireland here, and the coming of the Gael to Ireland - possibly with the Milesians, but maybe not. And as we've seen, this ran from 500 BCE to about 400 CE.

There was a big shift in the culture, and there is record of 3 tribes, observed by foreign writers and visitors, those who had heard stories from Ireland: the Brigantes, the Manapii, and the Coriondi. Modern scholars speak of an Irish Dark Age at this time, where it looks like the land stagnated both culturally and economically under the new iron order.

Well, they were losing their contact with the Otherworld, weren't they, after the Tuatha Dé Danann went back through the Sidhe, the

Mounds, and left this world to its fate?

Not all the Otherworld Beings abandoned them though. A few remained to oversee the human world; to help, to meddle, to guide, to advise, to feed.

And some remain here yet...

14

The Three Sisters

Faolín sighed and shifted her weight, earning herself kicks from her sisters, still sleeping, for her trouble. How could they sleep on this day?

But this was their way, to sleep the day and emerge in darkness, through darkness, to the world beyond. On this night of nights. Full of restless energy, Faolín rose as quietly as she could, though not quietly enough to spare her another sleepy kick from the eldest of the three. She left the chamber and sought her father.

Airiteach was tight in talks with his Draoí so she waited, her mind shifting from one topic to the next, fleet darts of thought that would not settle or sink in. At last he was finished, and she slipped in to wait by his great seat, until he turned and noticed her presence. His great brow broke clear of its darkened demeanour when his golden eyes rested on his youngest daughter, his heart's joy.

Just as was their way, they spoke of the night's work ahead, for though Faolín was youngest of the daughters of Airiteach, she was the cleverest and most conscientious. She had earned her father's respect, and his trust too, on many occasions when their work in the Other World may have gone very differently, had it not been for Faolín's quick wit and cunning.

Right then though, her head was not concerned with the ancient pact, the agreement that kept the world borders clear. For although her family had been charged with collecting the pact tribute for as long as the Elders could remember, it was what came after that inspired her eyes to light.

The Great Revel. Back in her own world, senses washed clean of the filth of her necessary journey, she got to stay here in her kingdom, for another whole year, and best of all... the music! The lights, the dancers, and the wondrous magic of music stirred her like nought else could.

Last night, when she and her sisters had ventured to the Other World for their first foray, she had heard an unusual thing, for that place. The harper Cas Corach had called the sisters and entranced them with his playing, for a short time. Their senses were too fine tuned for his sometimes fumbling fingers, he lacked the finesses of her own folk... but for one such as he, it was extraordinarily lyrical. Perhaps they would meet again this night, for she would enjoy to experience more of his talent.

Eventually, her sisters slouched from sleep, still grumpy and sniping at each other, but gradually that wore off and the excitement of the Wild Hunt grew upon them. They relished it more than she, truth be told, though there was a certain something to be said for the thrill of the chase, the power of thumping loam pounded by paws and claws.

When the time came, Airiteach released his daughters, and their pelts picked up a coating of clay mud as they sleeked through darkness of cave and stone, through to the world of men – the Other World than theirs...

Emerging, her middle sister first picked up the smell of prey beasts. Not far from the entrance and sitting downwind, their stupid bleating a clarion call through the gloom of Samhain night. The three followed the trail, moving as one, until cresting a rise they came again upon the human harper Cas Corach, sitting in the lee of an ancient mound of men.

When they appeared to him, he began to play, and called to them to come, to listen.

With soft words he spoke, timing speech to the enchanting notes he plucked on strings of finest metal wire. He sang the wolf sisters of the beauty that only human ears could hear, and convinced them to change form, all the better to hear him with. Faolín, the keenest, saw no harm, but when all three shifted, sat relaxed and trusting, the warrior Caílte stepped forth with Samhain spear and ran the sisters through from breast to breast, then took their heads before the last breath died, with one swing and sweep of sword.

And so the ancient pact was broken by the ignorance of men, with much more to the record than has made the history books... but sure, they're all stories for another day.

15

The Great Queen

She wore the mantle of power about her. A fine red woman is she; a sea of bright copper hair flowing down her back, red eyebrows on her high clear forehead, and a red cloak rippling down to the ground behind her, between the two poles of the chariot on which she stood. Pulling the chariot was a massive horse of chestnut red, but single footed, with the harness pole driven up through his body and stopped with a wedge on his brow. Her companion wore his own red cloak, and drove the massive red cow before him with a forked hazel staff, and not a single word or sound.

Cú Chulainn stepped out with a challenge, for all the cows of Ulster were under his care.

"This cow does not belong to you", says the woman, "nor to your friends or your family, nor to anyone you know. This task is too great for you Cú Chulainn, step away."

The Champion of the Uliad asked why it was the woman who speaks to him, and not the man?

"The man is 'cold wind and much rushes', as you would speak it", says she, "and I am 'little mouth edged, equally small hair, short splinter, much clamour', in your tongue".

"Do ye make a fool of me?", says the champion, and sprang up onto her two shoulders, planting his spear to her head. "Tell me your true name, woman!".

"It will not go well for you, if you do not remove your weapon from my very head and step away".

A slow smile spread over scarlet lips, and she says she is well skilled in the spells of satire, and she has brought this particular cow, on this particular day, as a fee for a master-poem. "Here, let me sing for you, warrior boy..." and she sang him a song of great insult, that so enraged him he twisted and turned throughout, his lips flecked with froth and spittle as he danced, the blood fury beginning to boil in his veins. He sprang again at the chariot, full ready now to strike at will and burn in the consequences, but found nothing before him. The chariot, the cow, the man and the woman had all disappeared from his sight.

Cú Chulainn turned again through empty air, bewildered, and in the shape of a great black bird on a bough he recognised her, the queen of danger, and as powerful in magic, and cried out – "If I had known it was yourself, that is not how we would have parted".

He heard her voice then, in his mind and on the wind both, and she told him that she is the guardian of Death, and would be there to preside over his own. She had brought that cow from the Sidhe of Crúachán, to meet with King Daire's Brown Bull, and Cú Chulainn had only until the calf in her belly turned a yearling to live. For that was when the Cattle Raid of Cúailnge would begin, and that was when he would die.

She warned that she would appear to him as an eel, to twist his legs like a noose as he fought in the ford. She warned she would appear as a grey wolf, and strip a stripe of flesh from his left hand over to his right. And she warned she would appear to him after as a white heifer with red ears, and bring with her a hundred other cattle with the same Otherworld colours as she, to drive together into the lake as he fought a man who was his equal, and take the very head from his shoulders.

Cú Chulainn mocked and jeered her, threatened he would injure her each time she came and never grant the healing of it after, but he spoke only to empty air, for she had departed back to fair Crúachán, leaving him to his pride, and the knowledge of his remaining time.

It wasn't the last he'd see or hear of the Great Queen Mórrígan... but sure, they are all stories for another day.

16

The Curse of Macha

Sometimes a Goddess fancies a change. Immortality can get awful boring after a time.

So it was with the Goddess Macha. She decided she wanted a home, friends of her own, a family... and that's how she ended up on the doorstep of a wealthy merchant in the mountains of Mourne. She knocked, asked to speak to him in person, and when he arrived down to greet her she made her proposal. She would bring wealth, prosperity, and abundance to his household (being a Goddess definitely has its perks), but in return she wanted a quiet life – to live out her days undisturbed, as a mortal. So he had to promise her privacy, and secrecy, and respect, and the love would come later, she was sure. And so he did. She turned thrice sun-ways on his step to seal the deal, and stepped into his life as a mortal wife.

The years trundled on and his household prospered, as she had promised it would. She brought abundance and wealth to his life, as she had promised she would. Love even bloomed, and she became pregnant, as is wont to happen when a man and a woman are in love. The merchant rose in status, and he began to receive invitations for them both to attend all the feasts, and all the fairs – invitations which she always declined, but he attended.

Unfortunately, his appetites grew right along with his status, and he began to feast and fair too much, eating and drinking until the wee small hours, and sometimes not even bothering to go home between events. Macha didn't mind too much; she kept herself busy, and was delighted when the physician told her she was carrying not one baby, but two – twins!

One month, near the end of her pregnancy, her husband was off again at one of his fairs. This was a big one: the Samhain festival at the court of the King. The merchant paid his tributes and tithes, ate his fill (and more) in the camp kitchens, and contented himself with wandering around the fair grounds, chatting to people he knew, looking through stalls and market tents, watching the competitive events, gaming for profit or loss... and of course drinking. Lots of drinking.

He sat eventually, content to watch the horse racing, and soon there was a cackling crowd, placing wagers on which would win. After a heavy loss, perhaps to salvage some part of pride perceived lost, the wine-soaked sot began to boast that as fast as those horses were, his own wife could out-run any one of them. Even the horses of the King himself, which were known to be the best of the best.

Now, it didn't take long for this boast to reach the ears of the King himself: for his horses represented his rightful rule, and any slight on them was a slight on his very kingship. He insisted the woman be fetched, and be made to race against the best horse of his stable. Warriors went out, Macha was made travel, and was told she would race the next day (as it was a three day festival). She bawled and cursed her husband - and his drunken, pounding, head - all through the night, but it was no use. She was stood in front of king and crowd first thing in the morning, with the horse lined up next to her. She sweated and swore, for the pressure was doing strange things to her heavily pregnant body, and it looked like mother and babies were in serious distress, to anyone with eyes to see.

The king held firm, and she was made to race – but before she did, she cursed every single man of Ulster, to nine generations on, with a spell that gave each and every one of them the pains of labour and childbirth, to strike them whenever Ulster was under attack.

She raced, and she won, but the exertion brought on the birth and she died there at the finish, screaming her curse to the last breath.

This is why the Ulster men were in bed each time their province needed them, and it caused a great many problems for them I can tell ya... but sure, they are all stories for another day.

17

Amergin and Ellen (not a love story...)

A shiver. By the Gods it was cold in those bushes, and getting damper by the minute. The heavy moon hung above, illuminating the landscape; but full dark would have suited his purpose better for sure. He wrapped his wool cloak tighter round him, remaining crouched, and watching.

Shuffling noises filtered up from behind him, an occasional cough. You might mistake it for the sleep sounds of beasts in the fields, if you didn't know there were 50 Ulster warriors concealed around and about. It was Amergin Mac Eccit who would face the beast alone though, when it came, as was the Chief Poet's duty. Looking out through the leaves that covered his position, he could see the entrance to the blasted cave; Uaimh na gCat, the Cave of the Cats.

It hadn't sounded too difficult, when King Conchobar had asked him first to consider a trip to Rathcroghan. Sitting in the great hall, warmed by a roaring fire and a belly full of roasted pig, watching his wife tend their infant son, Conall. Conor had timed it well and, with a few skins of wine already inside him, Amergin had easily agreed to travel to Connacht and take care of the little problem that sallied forth from their cave every Samhain. Ellen Trechend, following hot on the heels of an angry swarm of copper-red birds, emerging through the gateway between this world and the other – a gargantuan bird creature with three heads.

He'd never really liked birds. Pooping and chirruping and waking a man up of a morning when he'd only be trying to get a few hours sleep past the dawn... a sound. A long low whumpf, and a blast of warm moist air.

His skin felt slickened by the contact as it passed over his crouching form. More noises, a sense of pressure in the atmosphere. The night took a breath of anticipation and... whoosh. They were out and pouring forth from the darkness, spreading out like a copper stain on the land. The blood spill of the Otherworld, they came; a stream, a flow of deep red, and everywhere they passed the lush green landscape seemed to shrink and shrivel.

The ground shook. Amergin watched, fascinated, horrified, as the pestilent swarm spread through the countryside, their taint spreading across the ground with their passage. The ground shook again. It was coming.

In a daze, he stood, for what use was cover now? The very cave mouth trembled with what was to come, the trees rocked and groaned, the men behind him stayed silent and still. Eyes pinned to the gateway, Amergin the Poet began to gather strength. Not earth energy, for this creature was from the earth. Not sky energy, for a bird would eat that all up. Not fire, for it was said the creature's three mouths would open and flames would spit and fly at its will. But water? Amergin spied the ground between his position and the cave mouth, and watched for the shimmer of moving water as the ground shook. There, a shallow pool of ground water. He stood back from it, bait, a visible target for the creature.

Unfolding from the ground it came, rising, until he thought it could rise no more, and then three pairs of burning eyes over three identical razor beaks, and two great wings unfolded, their feathered ends tipped with barbs and spikes. Ellen Trechend towered over the Poet, who stood calmly. Waiting.

He thought of his sea journeys, in a tiny boat amid a vast empty ocean, but not the expanse of it – his focus instead was on the depth. Leagues of endless downward darkness. The creature advanced, screeching and spitting in fury, and Amergin waited. He heard the first splash of a clawed talon foot meeting the water. It made a dive toward him, sounds of rage moving to confusion as it suddenly felt a lot wetter than expected. Then the gateway Amergin had opened - connecting this shallow ground water to the deep, dark, bottomless sea - swallowed Ellen Trechend completely. Amergin smiled again.

The brave men of Ulster had many more adventures in Connacht after that, but sure they are all stories for another day.

18

River Woman

The finest bull, a rich deep black... well, not the finest perhaps. That particular party came later, with the brown and the white. But for now, a bull the black colour of a beetle's back, of deep river clay.

And that is where the River Woman's tale began...

The Dagda's woman slipped from his arms as he slept, for there was work to do. Always more work, but he had well earned his rest, and she needed him not for this.

Changing form slipped to her easily, as she shifted to – not a crow today, a Raven – and as she flew, she picked up others who seemed alike. They were telling her things as they alighted; interesting things, fascinating things. But she flowed her form again away from their wisdom and took on the horrid, phantom hawthorn aspect she enjoyed inhabiting for this work.

Growing her body, cycling through the embodiment of úath: the concepts of horrible, horrid, terrible terror, great dread, a spectre, a monster, a phantom, hawthorn tree, cold, earth and clay... they all sat in her mind for moments and blended together to create a fitting form for the Great Queen, going about her work in this world.

Then she went to find the right bull, a bull of cattle-rich Buchet, above in the fields by Crúachán. The most important bull, for now.

He didn't want to be off, to leave his submissive herds, but through the Sidhe ar Chrúachán they travelled swiftly together to Tara, her and the black bull, and then on to Óiriu's flat moorland heath. Furious was that swarthy, wild, clay coloured beetle of a bull, and so many times did he try to slip her determined grasp, that she named him Slemon – slippery – and sure wasn't that the name that stuck to that patch of land ever since?

But he did cover the cow, and so was done the work she had come to do, setting in motion the turning of tidings that would inexorably lead to gathered hosts and grave mounds.

Such was the work, and her work to do and get done. As it ever was.

The beetle black bull she left right there, demented and undefeated, thinking no more on him as she travelled swiftly back through the Sidhe to Crúachán.

Perhaps she wouldn't have given it another thought ever, since the proper pieces were in place, but as she emerged from the harmonious Cave of Crúachán, the Ravens landed in front of her with news. Voice had carried them a tale, predicting great feuds – of a pure woman who had been wronged, and a horrid Queen who was terrifying the land, stealing from a noble sturdy cow-lord. They had taken care of the serving-boy with the voice – he lay felled beyond in Cada's Nook – but the red-headed and great sized woman, that beloved companion to Buchet, was coming to the Sidhe for an iron-theft, for she thought she had the right, and the might.

Of course the woman didn't know the work, she didn't understand the way the worlds worked... and yet she thought to take it on herself to challenge the Mórrígan Mórda? With an iron-theft, from her fit abode?

It couldn't stand, and already the story of a bright, pure woman fighting an evil queen was spreading in the minds of men. Who else might think to wander through the worlds, believing their concerns or wisdom to be greater than the Great Queen?

It couldn't stand.

And so when Odras arrived, determined and fierce, to work her way through the shapely Sidhe of Crúachán, through the wilderness and under the hawthorn, to the great phantom hall – the shadow spectres shifted, and she found the cold was rising from the earth and clay. Her brow wrinkled in the dark, her mind grew numb and her breathing shallow. She couldn't stand, as the Mórrígan's magic worked up through physical flesh and she let sleep overcome her in the depths. She couldn't stand.

Between the worlds, the Great Queen worked. She sang the instruction over the sleeping body, chanting with fierceness unabated, without remission, with vehemence unabating, not allowing herself pause or reflection. Every diligent incantation was magical, each swift spell was sorcery.

Shifting her then to the scald crow shape of Slieve Baune, whispering sagacious words in the cold oak wood of that mighty mountain, the Mórrígan moved, and the spirited woman melted away.

Flesh became fluid, fresh clear water began flowing like Segais, a sleepy stream. Like any pool unnoticed without memorial stone, she slipped silently through the mountains – now a sweet-tasting greenish stream with no power of victory, for what chance had she?

That's not the only time the Mórrígan used her magic to gain a greater cause... but sure, they're all stories for another day.

19

The Sorcery of Scáthach

She knew the Boy had to leave.

It was past time, and his influence beyond disruptive.

He had crossed the Bridge of Pupils and earned his place, that much was true, but the rest... Her lips pursed tight. Least said, soonest mended, she thought.

Knowing his weakness for centering himself in every story, she had determined to find and tell him his place within this one. This seemed good to Scáthach, and so she had prepared the ritual to reveal.

Entering the chamber, she took first the food of the Sidhe. Chewing slowly on the raw red flesh of a hound, as had seemed appropriate for this occasion, she took the mound of chewed flesh from her mouth and placed it on the floor behind her chamber door - linking her bodily to the boundary stones of the space, the between place there.

The chant, taught to her by her mother, and then later again by her first lover, was building in her body, thrumming through her muscles and roiling round her belly, before making its way to her chest, to her throat, and boiling up, out, over the lips kissed by both of those women as they shared the chant with her, all those years before.

Opening her mouth, she connected her inside with the outside, matter with energy, the past with the present, as she sang the spells of old in the honour of her Gods.

Calling them, those who were her Gods, her Guides, her Guardians. Connecting them.

Feeling them, hearing them, seeing them – she was full of their sound and song as she lay down in the centre of the circular chamber. Trusting the island guards who stood outside, the women with whom she shared this practice, those for whom she had stood her sacred duty in turn, she arranged her form in place.

Her two palms rested on her two cheeks, crossed at the wrist to deflect and protect from her mouth as she slept. This kept the *Imbas Forosnai*, the words of prophecy and power, secure and safely together – forming and gestating inside her flesh - until she was to open her mouth again and allow the enlightenment to manifest in this world.

She stayed that way for all of the days and nights that were required. Until she was ready, until she was full of the knowledge, until that knowledge was right and ready for illumination.

And then Scáthach signalled for the Boy to enter her chamber.

And then she spoke...

> *Welcome, weary but victorious,*
>   *All-conquering, warlike, cold-hearted,*
>   *Come so that help may be given to you!*
>   *There will not be a foretelling without a chant,*
>   *there will not be a chant without a beholding.*
>   *About this warrior of single combat*
>   *awaits great danger.*
>   *Being alone for a long time during the cattle raid of Cooley*
>   *you will be dissipated,*
>   *from fighting the warriors of Cruachain.*
>   *Heroes will be saved by you; necks will be broken by you.*

Against the backstroke of Sétanta's blade,
blood will flow.
Bloody battle will sound over long distances,
spear points will shatter bones.
Wooden palisades will enclose the mighty horns of cows.
An aspen club with goodly edge will testify
to warrior feats and token flesh.
Cows from Brega will be stolen.
Hostages will swear by their people.
For a fortnight a third of the country will be full of tears,
cattle will go unherded about the roads.
A sorrowful single warrior will be against the host.
It will be difficult, to be sure, there will be a long sigh of lament.
The blood will drive a red pestilence onto many shields
of alderwood, and onto much weaponry;
The women will be red-eyed.
The battle-field will be red with the clash of weapons.
Ravens will eat well on flesh,
scald crows will traverse the ploughland.
Very strong kites will be encountered.
Portions of herds will be stolen through fierceness.
A large number will be led away for the great host,
a large amount of blood without flesh, will be spilt
on account of Cú Chulainn.
You will suffer injurious wounds.
You will slay a large number of unfortunate heroes.
The mill house of the lord will be plundered.
A destructive rout will bring great ruin to everyone
in Magh Muirthemne, during the wounding game.
The fiery hero will perform great deeds
against the Plunderers.

THE SORCERY OF SCÁTHACH

Performing cold deeds with dreadful shouting –
thus the feat-performing hero goes.
There will be weeping, a company of women will be wounded.
Medb boasts of destruction to Ailill.
A sick bed awaits you;
Thy face against cruelty and fierceness.
See the white-horned bull roar against the
Brown Bull of Cooley.
It will drive the wood of your ever-keen valour.
The learned son of red spear points will strike
a blow, curved and long.
Your journey will be lonely and without support.
Weakness is the cause that lays you low.
Arise, fully armoured one,
shapely in the art of many combats,
striding, raiding, oppressive,
arise in full force to the land of Ulster,
go to your Ulster maidens!
Weary, wounding warrior,
with your strong-shafted, effective, curved spear,
your brave blade will paint
in dark masses of black blood.
The Scot will know your name.
Screams and cries of a winter night,
Aífe and Úathach will lament you.
Your beautiful body laid low
by ingenious sleep making spells.
Three years on full thirty
will be the length of your power over your enemies.
Thirty years I boast
the power of your ever-keen deeds.

> *Beyond that I do not add,*
> *beyond that your life is not related.*
> *Among a troop of triumphant women*
> *your life will be short, this you will recognize.*
> *I bid you farewell.*
> *Welcome, weary but victorious.*[1]

It's not the last we'll hear of a prophetess trying to have fair dealings with the Boy.... but sure, they're all stories for another day.

---

[1] Prophecy Translation from: 'Cú Chulainn, an Iron Age Hero', by Daragh Smyth, pp. 44-46, Irish Academic Press (2005).

20

The Pillow Talk

There was a time then, that Queen Medb of Connacht, and her husband Ailill, were lying abed together, and for some reason (and sure we don't have to be going into exactly why that reason might be), he was feeling rather pleased with himself.

He's lying there, on the royal pillow, looking around at the sumptuous bed chamber, and he says - thinking out loud like: "She's a well off woman that's a rich man's wife".

Medb begins to ponder this, in an objective sort of a way, and may even have been about to agree, until it struck her who he was talking about. Propping up on one elbow, looking down on Ailill, she asks him to what, exactly, was he referring? When he opines that she herself was better off that day than the day he first took her... well, that's when things start to get serious.

Medb reminds her husband of her ancestry then and there, and that although her father, the King of Ireland, had six lovely daughters, she herself was the noblest and seemliest of them all. She was the goodliest of her sisters in bounty and gift-giving, in riches and treasures, and indeed the best of them in battle and strife and combat.

She commanded many thousands of men in her household guard, and claimed for herself one fifth of Ireland, the province of Connacht, and therefore was she known as 'Medb of Crúachán'.

Her suitors were many, the sons of kings all, and she refused them to a man. For she demanded a singular bride-gift, such as no woman before her had ever required of the men of Erin, namely, a husband without avarice, without jealousy, without fear. And isn't it a good thing for Ailill that she found those particular traits so lacking in him, and took him on? A man dependant on a woman's maintenance; that's what he was, says she.

"Not so", says he! Not at all, indeed.

And it was very important to get this settled, for who had brought the wealth got to make the decisions. Now that it had been put to Medb she couldn't let it lie, or she would lose her standing, and perhaps be nothing more than a pleasant decoration about the palace of Crúachán. And so she raised the chamber, and the household, and insisted on a full count, then and there, of all they both owned.

It began with the least of their possessions, their pails and their cooking cauldrons and their iron-wrought vessels, their jugs, their bowls, and their eared pitchers were all fetched out to them. Then their rings and their bracelets and their thumb-rings, and all the golden treasures were brought to them, and their clothing, all the colours, textures and styles. They were evenly matched, and a fine sight they made, all laid out.

Then their numerous flocks of sheep were led in from fields and plains, counted and compared, and found to be equal, of like size, of like number. They did find a fine ram over Medb's sheep, and she got a little excited at the sniff of victory, but a corresponding ram was found with Ailill. Their horses were brought, and numerous droves of swine, all numbered and counted and claimed. Even down to the chickens, they matched like for like.

Until they brought the cattle. These were carefully counted, and recounted, for they were equal in size, equal in number... except there was a special bull, a calf of the Queen's herd, and Fionnbheannach, 'the Whitehorned', was his name. But he (the calf grown to a fine bull), had apparently thought it no honour to be in a woman's possession, and had left for the King's herd.

So after all, it was the same to Medb as if she owned not a pennyworth, because she had no bull to match the White amongst her cattle. She let the exhausted household retire at that - though her husband, we may be sure, didn't get his head back on the royal pillow that night. Queen Medb certainly didn't leave it there, like a good and dutiful wife might.

But sure, they are all stories for another day

21

The Prophetess

Medb turned in her chariot, to survey the assembled armies across the plains of Crúachán.

"Everyone leaving a lover or friend today will curse me", says she, "for they gathered for me". She raised her arm to signal setting off, with the men around her mad to be on the move, but faltered as she saw a single chariot approach from the South, up from the Cave of the Cats, portal between the Otherworld and this.

A singular woman was driving, pulled by two strong stallions as deep a blue-black as midnight without moon. She was young but full grown, with two tresses of yellow hair bound about her head, while the third flowed down her back, brushing her calves behind. Her speckled cloak shimmered as she drove across the plain, fastened secure by a gold clasp at her shoulder, and she was armed as she came. More gold was around her hooded tunic embroidered with red, and the clasps on her sandals.

As she drew closer they saw more clearly her true beauty, for didn't she have a broad fair brow and a narrow, elegant jawline, with her beauteous fine black eyebrows and long lashes casting shadows in the noonday sun right across her smooth cheeks. Her teeth were like jewels set between full scarlet lips, but it was her eyes that brought gasps from the gathered men – as she stopped her chariot and looked upon them they saw a universe of grey, green, blue and gold, with a triple black iris in each.

"What is your name?" Medb said to the woman before her.

"I am Fedelm Banfhile, the woman poet and prophetess of Crúachán", says she. "I've come lately from learning verse and vision in Alba".

"Have you *Imbas Forosnai* then, the Light of Foresight? Tell me what is in store for us now".

Fedelm cast her Otherworldly eyes across the host that were there from all the provinces in Ireland. Medb scarce breathed while she waited for what the woman had to say. Then she turned sad-faced to her Queen.

"I see it Crimson, I see it Red".

This was not what Medb had hoped to be hearing, so she drew herself up and proclaimed;

"Sure that can't be true! I've had messengers back fresh from Ulster who swear that the King Conchobar and all his fighting men lie abed with the curse of a goddess upon them, to suffer the pangs of child-birth even until we attack their homes and steadings. Look again woman".

Again Fedelm cast her eyes across the plains of Crúachán, teeming with bright life and strong energy.

Again she told Medb; "I see it Crimson, I see it Red".

"But it must be false!" says Medb, disbelieving. "All the Kings of Ireland have sent troops to this Táin, even Conchobar of Ulster, as Fergus and the three thousand exiles sit with us waiting to attack their very own homeland".

Without hesitation this time, Fedelm proclaimed as she saw; "I see it Crimson, I see it Red".

"Wrath and rage and red wounds are common when battle is taken, and it is surely this which you are seeing with your strange eyes", says Medb, but the prophetess cut her off sharply;

"I see the battles – a red-blonde man, young, with much blood around his belt and a hero halo around his head. Who he is I cannot tell, the hound is with him and he shines with a power that is great and terrible. It warps his form and twists his mind to fight and frenzy, I see the whole host coloured crimson by his hand.

Total ruin at his touch, torn corpses, your warriors dead because of him, the Hound of Ulster".

Without another word, Medb raised her arm and signalled the men to march and move, riding to the forefront in her chariot alongside her husband Aillill.

"What did the prophetess say of this?" he asked, for word had spread.

"She said nought awaits us in Ulster but a boy and a hound", says she, restless eyes not meeting his.

That's not the last we'll hear of Queen Medb in Connacht, but sure, they are all stories for another day.

22

The Cave of the Cats

Way, way back in the world, Queen Medb at Rathcroghan in Connacht was not the best of friends with King Conchobar at Navan Fort in Ulster, to say the least of it. They were always arguing and threatening, robbing one oul' bull or another, and the both of them always trying to outdo the other.

On one particular day, King Conchobar up North was getting an awful headache, with his three best champions arguing and bickering over who was the best of them, for really real. It'd been going on for a while, and he had enough of the lot of them. He hatched a cunning plan, designed to move the problem (his own problem, but sure we'll not focus on that for now) right down into the lap of Queen Medb. He went and told the three warrior bucks, after he'd pulled them off each other during a particularly vicious looking brawl, that as soon as they'd cleaned up their cuts and bruises they were to all head off down to the court at Rathcroghan, where Queen Medb, in all her gracious wisdom (snicker snicker, says he) would be only delighted to decide which of them was the one and only true champion of the Northern court.

The first Medb knew of it was from the scouts up on her palace walls; the shout went out as soon as the first plume of dust was spied far in the distance across the plains, and as each chariot came closer, she was able to figure out who was heading her way by the descriptions they were shouting down. She was well familiar with these lads, sure she had to be in her position, and was there to greet each one as they arrived to her gates – Laegaire Buadach, Conall Cearnach, and Cú Chulainn.

She got the story out of them quickly enough and her brain began to scramble for a way of getting herself, and her household, out of the danger they now found themselves in. For the lads had been promised a sure and final answer to their on-going ego problem. If they didn't get that answer, there'd be hell to pay.

But if they did get their answer, there'd still be hell to pay – sure the two named losers wouldn't be happy about that at all! So she separated them quickly, sent each to his own little house a mile or so apart from each other, and told them she'd send their dinner in after them. They were to sleep in their houses tonight, and she'd make her decision in the morning, before they went back home to Ulster.

When they were all settled in, she had her servants prepare their food, while she paid a visit to the Cave of the Cats... and came back out with company. Delivered along with each would-be champion's dinner was a giant, stone-headed monster cat from the Otherworld, that she'd brought through inside in the cave. The doors were locked and the lads left to see how they'd fare overnight.

When the servants went to check in the morning, they found that Laegaire Buadach was gone altogether, and the cat had his dinner all eaten up and was asleep in his bed. Conall Cearnach had managed to stay in the house, at least, but his dinner was eaten too, and the cat asleep below in his bed. But when they'd looked in on Cú Chulainn, they found him in a stand-off with the giant cat – his sword planted on the creatures head and the pair of them snarling at each other all night. The dinner lay between them, untouched, and the bed remained un-slept in.

Queen Medb met each of them individually, and gave them a wrapped chalice in secret, telling them to go and show their King the prize, and he would know which of them was the true champion. And they all went off satisfied, Laegaire with a bronze, Conall with a silver, and Cú Chulainn with gleaming gold.

So that is how the brave Queen Medb turned the tables on King Conchobar, and it's certainly not the only time they were at odds. But sure, they are all stories for another day.

23

A Form Very Excellent

Grey eyes regard me back from the pool by which I sit. The still water shows dappled greens above my head, a broad sky stretched beyond. I look beneath and search within, and find myself in form and function for this time, this place.

Legs to bear a body, feet to meet this earth. The one I seek will respond to a pleasing form, and how to make it so is soon told. Female in figure, so curves here, and here. Shoulders slim, and fair, but solid. Legs lengthened, with strength and grace to thigh and calf... no, not that calf. A human leg calf, for the bovine kind comes not yet. Human calves on human legs, there. And a proud arch to the foot, curved high to step light, to play and dance with the wind as I walk this realm. But that is mine, for me.

A form very excellent, and a face, with this shape and that angle, and skin so clear and pale – a face of surpassing beauty. A dress of every colour, for how can I declare for one and wear it well? Besides, his attention span is short and his mood fickle. If it shifts, like this, moulding the curve here and allowing the flow there, and the colour is not quite the same in any place, or when he looks the second time... There.

Formed and clothed. And how to approach?

I know his mind, and I know his pride. I wear what he expects to see, so I shall speak what he expects to hear. I am a princess, Cú Chulainn, the daughter of a king. I have loved you from afar, Cú Chulainn, for your reputation stretches across the land. I fell in love with you, Cú Chulainn, upon hearing of your fame, and I bring my treasures and my wealth for you to claim.

If it is timed for when he is distracted and sore, timed for when he is starving and stressed. Then shall he refuse my aid, and well, I will have made a just and goodly offer, sure.

And then, we shall see. Then we will know.

* * *

Cú Chulainn threw the broken bodied Láiríne from the river, out into the waiting arms of Lugaid. Mangled as he now was, Lugaid was grateful for the breath his brother still drew, and departed the battle to begin his care.

The air was thick with the stench of the shit he had squeezed from the body of his foe, and the water of the ford was clogged and choked with his dung so no good flow or freshness could be found. Cú Chulainn climbed to the bank and began to gather handfuls of sweet grass to wipe and clean, his weapons first and then his form, as best he could. Disgusted, he shook his head and turned from the water to find a young woman walking toward him.

And oh, she was radiant to his eyes, as pure and clean as sunshine warming a meadow's brook. Embarrassed by his distorted form, as ever, in the presence of true beauty, his mood darkened further when he saw the scene as she must be seeing it. He smelled it too, and himself within it.

When she spoke to him it was with a voice that would change the world, offering him her wealth, herself, as the daughter of a king... but sure, how could she want him true? How could she look at him, knowing her fairness of form, and speak of love to a man-child slathered in shite, standing by a river flowing with blood that he had spilled? And how could he spare the time now to find out what was real, even for a prize such as this?

"It is not a good time at which you have come to us, that is, our condition is ill, we are... starving. So it is not easy for me to meet a woman while I am in this strife", says he.

"I shall help you in it", offers she, and tilts her hip and tempts him, to be sure.

"No", says he, now sure. "It is not for a woman's body that I have come."

The Mórrígan smiled then, using the slick red mouth she wore that day. And using too that throat of rare beauty, she promised him she would return, in three forms, to hinder instead where she would have helped.

That was not the first, nor the last that Cú Chulainn felt her presence in his affairs, for she keeps her promises and does it well... but sure, they are all stories for another day.

24

In the Alps

Fraech, he was, a son of the Sidhe; boy-pet of the King of the Sidhe of Erin (that's what they called him, no word of a lie now).

He tended 12 cows of the Otherworld, each a pure ruddy red with ears of white, like snow settled upon them. But they were stolen away to the North of the North, across the oceans and into the Alps; so the bean sidhe Béfind - his mother, and the sister to Bóand – didn't she tell him that not only had his cows been taken, but the three sons he had and his own wife were all gone as well. If he was to go and get them though, said she, it'd cause much trouble to him, and sure she'd give him on other cows? He'd promised those cows to Medb for the cattle raid that was to come though, and so he had to head off and get them back. Plus, his wife and sons were kind of important to him too.

When he was up round the Mountains of Mourne, at Benna Bairchi to be exact, didn't he meet none other than the bould Conall Cearnach, the Victorious, and they got to talking. Fraech showed off his hawk, though he called it the wood-cuckoo, and the great hound he'd brought along, and there was great craic had with the three nines of young warriors that had come along for the raid. They were all grand lads and lasses. And he tells the quest to Conall, whose name means 'strong as a wolf', in the hopes that he'd join them too... sure it couldn't do any harm to have him along?

Now, Conall knows it's nothing lucky and much in the way of trouble that awaits them, and he says as much. But he also knows that it's important that it be done, and Fraech should indeed be focussing his mind there, for it's not all going to be played out in this physical world. This is where Conall was strong, and Fraech knew it. With their history, he also knew that Conall would help him any time they should meet, and so he did this time – agreeing to come along for the spin out. It was some spin though, with travelling over the sea and across the Saxon lands, over the next sea and across the lands of the Long-bards, until they found the mountains of Elpa. After a while there was a wee girl tending a herd of sheep away to the south of them, and they decided to leave their youths behind them so as not to be arriving down on top of her all in a warrior band, so the two lads set out to talk to her by themselves first. As is often the way, for the Irish do love to travel the world and ever has it been the same, it turned out that the girl's own Mammy was from Erin, so she knew she'd better help them as best she could, for the men of Erin didn't do well in that country, as she saw it, and they'd need the extra bit of luck she could pass along.

"This is a grim hateful land with troublesome warriors, who go on every side for carrying off cows and women as captives", she says. "And the latest thing they've brought back here is the cows of Fraech, son of Idath, from the west of Erin, and his wife, and his three sons. Here is his wife here in the house of the king, here are his cows in the country in front of you."

"Well now", says Conall, "this is none other than Fraech right here before you, and hasn't he been awful wronged? You should help us all you can for that now". All she had to offer though was advice, and it wasn't bad – there was a woman minding the cows who was from the men of Ulster, no less, and she'd help them surely if they told her of their errand.

Off they went then and found her easy enough, but when they told her what they were after she wasn't hopeful for their success, for there was a large serpent guarding the lios, the fort which lay part in this world and part in the other, and guarding the women there specifically. It was only when Conall Cearnach named himself specifically that she got all excited, threw her both arms around his neck and told him it was to him that the destruction of the fort had been prophesied.

She'd have to grease the wheels on that prophesy a little, for sure, but it was she who locked the lios each night, so that'd make things a wee bit easier. She warned them again of the serpent though, it would be their only real trouble there. It was not of their country, for sure, but several tribes had come from it. It'd bear caution.

Gathering their party, they attack the lios, and straight away Conall Cearnach is in battle with serpent. Its darts leap into his girdle, the crios belt he wears as a talisman and protection, and in the Otherworld, the real battle is fought in earnest. Patterns on the crios shift and twine, sinuous through the entanglement, weaving and working against the great serpent's strength. This is a powerful ancestor spirit, with many magics overlaid and worked through for many generations past. As Fraech and the youths are off saving the wife and the sons, and even plunder the gems and rescue a few of them oul cows while they're at it, Conall and the serpent come to an understanding – for though they can't do harm to one another, neither will he let it go... but when he agrees to release it, they are free and clear to travel home safely, and so they do.

He'd made a strong ally in that serpent, and there was more work to be done and roles to live up to, with it wrapped around his waist... but sure, they are all stories for another day.

25

Getting Well

The rain was writing itself onto her body, as she made her way from the mountain hut above, down the trail.

It wasn't the fat heavy drops that sometimes ganged up on you and landed plopping on your skin with that splash patter, forming the beat of miniature drums. No, it was one of the other types of water from the sky they were all so used to there, the one where you find yourself thinking 'Oh it's not really raining, just a grand soft day'... but within 2 minutes of being out in it you're walking through a wall of misty water and finding yourself thoroughly drenched, soaked through, with no clear sense of actually even having been rained on.

It was the kind of rain that snuck up on ya.

The lake below was drinking up the water, as she moved past the waterfall and down to pick her spot on the shore. Fire hardened spear gripped firmly in hand, she put her bare feet in the water over the smooth stones all along the edge, and waded out a while to stand, and wait.

Full of fish that lake was, she knew it well. But do you think even a one of them would wander past her waiting spear that time? Not in the 2 hours she stood, stock still with long practiced patience, the slick wet from above coalescing on her skin and finally forming a few drips to drop with a light occasional plink to the surface of the water.

Sighing then, she wondered if it was somehow her own inner upset that was frightening the lake fish away that day, for didn't her grandmother lie dying above in the hut, with not a thing any of them could do for her? Back on the shore, and at that point of wet and cold that any more time out in it doesn't pass you any mind, she wandered over to the well and the stream, with the thought of a prayer for sláinte, or siochán at least, for the woman she loved so well.

Sitting down by the deep well, she offered her prayer, and promised what she had to give if anything could be done for her grandmother, on that day or any other. And the water on her face then wasn't from above or below her, but welling up from deep within her; following the flow of feelings as it moved within her and found its own way out.

Movement by the shoreline caught the corner of her eye, and as she turned she saw a sight - a large eel was coming right to the well as she'd been praying, and her own mother had told her what that meant. As sure as anything, she knew that if she was praying at a holy well and she'd see an eel coming towards the well, it meant that the person she was praying for would be cured by the time she got back home. For certain that's what it meant!

So very pleased was she to see that eel coming, that she didn't even think of catching it for eating, and instead she laughed and thanked it and blessed it, with pure hope in her heart and joy on her lips she thanked it and blessed it out loud, and she meant it.

"Well sure it's a long time since I've been thanked or blessed", said the eel, and the girl near fell over with the full shock of hearing it speak to her. She wouldn't be a one given to flights of fancy though, and so it was that an acceptance that came on her quickly. Of course it was a magical eel - if it had the power to cure her half dead grandmother above, sure why couldn't it be talking to her down below here? The eel kept going as it was then, towards the well where it plopped in, and then they were both in slightly more of a comfortable situation... because seeing the protruding lower jaw and blunt teeth of the huge eel up close as it spoke to her was perhaps the most disconcerting part of the entire situation.

They talked a long oul while that day, and indeed, on other days too. The girl even brought her well recovered grandmother down to the lakeshore after all that, to give her own thanks and blessing upon the creature. As time went on it grew even larger, far beyond the usual size of one of its kind - perhaps because of all the attention and blessings, or perhaps because of the extra food the girl would share with it on the good days of plenty. The eel grew so large in fact, and lived so long in that lake nestled at the foot of the mountains, that much, much later it became known as a Peist, a serpent or a monster in the eyes and minds of those who came after, and claimed the lands and the lake for their foreign god.

But sure, they are all stories for another day.

26

Snow White Skin

Log fires chuffed smoke through the great hall, as a fierce wind blew through the chimneys. All were quiet that night. A curious air of melancholy had settled around dinner, and nothing seemed likely to shift the strain of it from King Conchobar's court where they sat.

Nessa, mother to the king, called for the royal storyteller Fedlimid Mac Daill, to spin a tale and lift the mood. But her woman said his wife was abed with the birthing pangs at last, and he paced the halls awaiting a cry from the babe and news that all would be well. At this, the Druid Cathbad pricked his old ears and roused himself to lay the bones, and see what manner of child would be born to the keep that night. Truth be told, he'd been uneasy since morning, and this might break the why of it at least.

The bones fell as usual, with their slashed line markings hither and thither on the skins, and only Cathbad knew the meanings they foretold. His sharp intake of breath was enough to perk King Conchobar, who looked on with curiosity as the Druid moved slowly deiseal around the skins, to see the thing that was told from all sides.

"What do you see old friend, that wrinkles your brow all the more?" says the King, as Cathbad studied the patterns how they fell. Gathering the bones, he made his way to the throne, though the whole hall was letting a low curious buzz by then to know what he had to say.

"The daughter born at court this night will be the greatest beauty that Ulster ever saw," says the Druid, low into Conchobar's ear, "but she'll cause more pain than any before her too".

"Great beauty brings its own problems, in truth, but yet its own rewards. Did you see her face and form? Describe her as she is grown," says the King. And Cathbad did. He told of her grace and lyrical voice, her cream fair skin and her luscious form... and then he told of the kings and lords who'd go to war for her, and the three greatest warriors of Ulster who would live in exile for the sake of her. But sure hadn't the King stopped really listening with the description of lush beautiful form, and, in his ardour, commanded the child be taken and raised in his sight. He could wait.

Cathbad repeated the warnings, the dire predictions of doom around the girl's life, and eventually enough got through that Conchobar commanded the child be raised away from contact, by a trusted nursemaid, Leabharcham. And so the crone took her and raised her, teaching her as best she could the skills and habits of royalty, knowing all the while full well that aging Conchobar would have her married and made Queen as soon as he saw fit.

Deirdre, they named her, and she grew to be everything Cathbad had described, and more. She was a kind girl, patient with age, though Conchobar's visits, increasing in frequency, rubbed her all wrong. She loved him not, though he was all the man she'd ever laid eyes on – she knew there had to be more and fairer than he.

The girl was allowed a modicum of freedom, in that wild place where she was reared, and so it was after 16 years, when out hunting one day, she shot down a crow that came in her path when her aim had been for the tree pigeon beyond. And as the bird lay bleeding on the snowy ground, Leabharcham came upon her, kneeling in the cold to gaze upon it.

"What is it child, what do you see that moves you so?"

"This," says Deirdre, "this is the sign of my life to come. I'll not rest ''til I find a man with skin white like the clear snow, hair as black as wing of crow, and lips that glisten the ruby red of fresh blood."

Now, it just so happened that Leabharcham knew such a man, and find him she did. All that had been foretold came indeed to pass... but sure, they are all stories for another day.

III

The Fenian Cycle

27

About This Time...

They say that Cormac Mac Airt was the High King at Tara, like his father (Art) before him... but I have me own doubts now, I must admit, on whether anyone just pulling out of the Tribal bedlam of the Iron Age could truly control and rule the whole island.

Was there ever even a High King in anything but name? How would that even work?! And why at Tara specifically, when there are other sites where the archaeology more strongly supports a bigger/wider footprint of leadership... it smells of Medieval romanticism to me, but I will admit a certain bias towards a certain Connacht stronghold, so maybe my own perception is a touch skewed. Let's leave it at that for now then, shall we?

Anyhow, that's when the Fenian Cycle is supposed to be set, or the Ossianic Cycle; named for Fionn Mac Cumhail (Finn Mac Cumaill), and his son Oisín, respectively. These tales revolve around Fionn and his warband Na Fianna, who held their ancient capital at Almu on the Hill of Allen, in County Kildare.

To date this now is a bit contentious.

Given the above, and what is 'known', we'll go with about the 300s or 400s CE - the cusp between the end of the Iron Age, the start of the

Early Medieval, and the coming of christianity to the island.

However, there are them that will tell you that to look at the Fenian tales, you'd think they were set in a much earlier time, when society wasn't settled into agriculture even, and the Fianna roamed the land as Hunter Gatherers. They'd ask you now, so they would, if we might be looking at a set of stories that go back those 10,000 years to the Mesolithic, and tell the tales of a time very long past.

Arra now, how would we ever know for certain anyway? Maybe the Irish have always been a bit wild, with bands of us roaming the landscape no matter what the farmers and townsfolk were doing or not doing. Maybe we have always had this grá, this passionate love for stories, and maybe we held onto the same ones for a very long time, taking the old seeds and growing new plants - whole vibrant gardens! - telling and retelling our stories to fit the times we find ourselves in.

Sure isn't that exactly what this very book is all about?!

28

By His Thumb

"You'll not have it from him quick enough now Caoilte, to get it in your gob and ate before he has that dagger to your throat and I've a mess to clean up."

The warrior Caoilte started guiltily, frowning at his chief across the low flames; for he had indeed been contemplating taking his companion's dinner, as he waved it round in front of him, gesticulating wildly as he told some oul story or another.

He stopped himself then from asking how Fionn had known his plan… sure didn't he have his thumb stuck between his teeth? Didn't he always do that, and catch them out at one thing or another?

With a grumbling voice that matched his still hungry belly, Caoilte first nodded across at Fionn to let him know he could stand off, there wouldn't be any trouble from him that night now, and then asked the Fianna leader, "How'd you get that gift anyway, of the knowing? I've heard a few different tales by now, but I'd hear your own, if you'd share it."

Taking a breath to speak, Fionn was interrupted by Cairbre, saying: "I heard a story on that now, so I did, and I can share it if you'd like?" And with a wry amusement for what the lad might have to say, he let him tell his tale...

"Back before my time now, it was, before you were you even," says Cairbre, "and ye were on the banks of the river Suir that time, and only after killing a big pig for the day's feeding. Oisin was set to boil it, and wasn't he attacked by something before he even knew it, with the whole pig gone clean out of his fair hands? He followed it then, on to the source of the attack, right up to the top of the Sidhe ar Feimhean, but it got inside and shut the door, and wasn't he left standing outside and scratching his head, and that was that.

Wasn't it yourself then, Caoilte, who was set to cook another pig on the second day, and the whole thing happened all over again? Straight up, same as before, only it was you coming back down after a wild chase over the mountain, to have the door slammed in your face at the Sidhe above."

Caoilte let a groan and shook his head sympathetically at that, sharing deeply both the memory and the recent frustration of having food so close to hand, but not in your belly. When he caught Fionn's eyebrow raised in his direction though, he shut up quick and went back to listening to the story.

"You went yourself to boil it then Fionn, using your spear hafts in the left hand, and with your other hand turning the pig on the points of the fork. Something clutched at it, sure enough, just as it was near finished the cooking. You gave the crathure a blow, but the point of your spear only just reached its back, but it dropped the pig at least. You didn't stop though, following along it's whole mad dash - seven times it jumped across the Suir with you back and forth the same!

You followed it back up the mountain then Fionn, up to the Sidhe cairn on top, so ya did, and just as the thing tried to slip back to the Otherworld, you lobbed your spear and killed it dead - broke its back, done and done.

But there was a woman there too, inside in the cairn, and she'd been giving out cups of a drink before, and sure didn't she try and close the door to the Sidhe, quick as a whip, til you thrust your hand in right after the path the spear had flown, and got your thumb stuck between the door and the post and kept the way open. Putting the thumb in your mouth, you heard them wail - What is that? Cúldubh has been killed! - and you let off some poetry or other that I wouldn't even start with trying to understand.

That's it though, isn't it? That's how you can have the Imbas Forosnai whenever you gnaw on your thumb... sure isn't half of it still stuck beyond there in the Otherworld?!"

The Fenian leader laughed then, leaning over the fire and gave it a poke of a stick, while they all sat and waited for him to confirm or deny the truth of the story that Cairbre had just told.

They might be still waiting, or he might have told them another tale then and there about his thumb, and the knowledge it held... but sure, they're all stories for another day.

29

The Ninth Wave

I sat on the shore, watching the dance and sparkle of sun on water, and seeing nothing. Nothing dances inside a heavy heart, nothing sparkles through a weary, worn spirit. I was nothing, then.

The great sea heaved its rhythm through my head regardless. The pattern of waves inserted into my mind, inciting me to notice, to follow, to count the waves. Each one lapped in, and out, with steady ebb and flow. I followed. In the cycle, one to eight were even, and then the ninth came. The ninth wave came each time; larger and longer, bolder and bigger, fine and free the ninth wave fell.

I watched each time. I felt it coming now, a familiar build through the order, and then the crash and boom, the expression of power and promise. The sun danced and sparkled on the water, a broad golden glitter, a pathway pulsing with each wave, and never clearer than on the ninth. Promise. The Land of Promise lay across the broad ocean, Tír Tairngire. It called to me, to come away, to follow the path across the sea and find my peace in promise.

And the ninth wave brought a distant shadow on the horizon, but when it fell to shore, the shadow passed. Each cycle brought the shadow closer - a smudge with the coming of the next ninth wave, and a shape with the show of the next. A silhouette, a figure, a woman. She stepped then across the golden glitter with the lightest of feet, calm and balanced as she rose and fell, moving to shore and nearer with each ninth.

Her face and form awoke me, my heart and spirit responding to the perfection of sheer Sidhe beauty. My eyes had never rested on such wonder before the vision of her approach. She strode the sea as a creature born to it, finding with each footstep a perfect wavelet crest on which to float. When she reached the sand, she stopped, the water bearing her weight without a touch of land beneath her. She beckoned me from my daze. When I stood in front of her, her radiance near blinded my eyes and I wanted more, I wanted the sight of her to be the last thing I ever did see.

Her name was Cliona, she said, as I stayed dumbstruck in her presence. Descendant of Lear, and daughter of Manannán, Keeper of Oceans. Her voice soothed my soul as the sound of gently lapping water, as the sound of a breeze sighing through seagrass. She came with the waves to answer my call, she said; to offer succour, to bring me to promise. I wanted that. I wanted to sit with her, to see her face, to hear her voice, to feel all that I felt in that moment for ever more. I wanted that with my heart, with my spirit, with all that danced and sparkled in her presence.

She lifted her hand and pointed along the shore. A currach lay there, up the way a bit and broken a bit, as it hadn't been treated yet for the season. I went and she watched as I pulled it over, and satisfied myself that it would float at least, across the golden pathway to get me to Tír Tairngire. I lifted and dragged the little boat down to the water's edge, to where she stood with waves licking her toes and heels, and I pushed it out into the sea, wading til it was born afloat, then climbing inside.

I watched her face as she kept pace with the craft, as the waves brought us away from land. I focused on her form as each ninth wave lifted us higher, pushed us farther along the path that disappeared rapidly as the clouds came down. I listened to her laughter as each ninth wave crashed each time onto the bow of the boat. My heart danced and my spirit sparkled as Cliona's ninth wave crushed my craft, bringing me to the promise and into her world.

That's not the last time one of us was brought to their world... but sure, they are all stories for another day.

30

The Sidhe at Keshcorran

Fionn MacCumhaill, leader of the noblest band of Irish warriors, the Fianna, sat on the hunting mound at Keshcorran, taking in the sights and sounds that made his heart most happy. His men were spread below him on this fine sunny day, ranging the fields and forests, their great hounds barking and baying around them as they brought down kill after kill. The Fianna would feast well that day.

Conaran however, who was the King of the Sidhe in those parts, was less than happy to see his old enemy in such a fine, untroubled mood. And with the rest of the Fianna busy hunting, he decided the time had come to do something about Fionn for once and for all. Three of Conaran's four daughters were nearby, although neither the men of the Fianna nor their chief could see a bit of them, because you never can see the Sidhe unless you are in their world, or they want you to see them in ours. The King called his brood – who were as ugly a bunch as you ever saw, and worse again – and told them what he wanted. Then, by his magical arts, he opened a door to their world in the side of the Sidhe mound on which Fionn was taking his ease. After a while, the warrior chief climbed down to join the hunting party below, and was astounded to see the three sisters sitting spinning in a cave that he was sure hadn't been there before he'd climbed up.

Now you couldn't call any of these Mná na Sidhe beautiful. Well, you could I suppose, but you'd be telling a lie if you did. Fionn though, was a curious sort, and wanted to see more - it might have been the whiskers he thought he could see on their faces? Whatever was driving him to it, he stepped inside the mound.

As soon as he passed the holly on the threshold, a weakness came over him, and he could no more lift his own arm than he could have lifted a whole mountain at the best of times. He tried to give the whistle that would warn the rest of the Fianna to danger, but he was so weak that all the sound he could make was a chuff like a baby falling asleep, and sure that'd warn nobody. He was bound by the sisters with every knot and tie they could think of, and as each warrior came looking for their leader and stepped inside the mound, the same fate befell them. The Sidhe mound was filled only with the sounds of gently chuffing babies, until every single man of them was captured and bound the same way.

But their dogs were not. As each man entered the mound, ignoring the warning signs in the search for his leader, his hound refused, and soon there was a great pack of barking, baying dogs gathered outside. Finally one of the warriors, the last of them left outside, had the sense to be cautious enough not to follow blind into danger. The hideous sisters watched Goll Mac Morna stand his ground outside, and decided that three against one was a fair enough fight for them to take him on. They were wrong, of course. Though it was hard fought, Goll managed to chop two of the three into halves and bits; so there were warts and twisted fingers on one side of him, gnarled toes and crooked noses on the other. Panting with the effort of it all, he extracted (in exchange for her life) the firm promise of freedom from enchantment for the Fianna from the last sister, who was so terrified by then that her whiskers were all atremble, on both the outside and inside of those livery lips.

She kept her honour, and released each of the warriors to sit out in the sunshine and shiver until their strength returned. The doings of that day did nothing to ease the enmity between Fionn and the Sidhe King Conaran, nor his remaining daughters of the Sidhe – nor even the animosity between Fionn and Goll Mac Morna.

But sure, they are all stories for another day.

31

The Magical Deer

It was a bright day, fair and cool, when Fionn was coming back towards the Dún after a morning's hunt in the woods beyond. His hounds, the cousins Bran and Sceolán, caught a scent on the wind and chased off towards cover, only to come back a wee while later, not hunting, but in company with a doe of such beauty and grace as to stop the heart in his chest, for wasn't he a man who appreciated the form and grace of such things?

The surprising thing though, was that his hounds lay down with the deer, and set up such a snuffling frolic round her that Fionn was straight over to investigate. He thought it'd be a shocking shame to kill such an unusual, elegant creature, and called the dogs away 'til they could set off home... only to be followed along by the doe herself. Being no stranger to odd happenings, he'd learned a long time before to just shrug and get on with things 'til they became clearer, so that's what he did.

Later that night, when he was alone by the fire in the great hall, a woman came to him whose limbs were suffused with a familiar elegance and grace and whose voice, when first he heard it, soothed a part of his soul that had been churning and raging without him even knowing it.

They talked long through the night, and he found that she was Sadbh, daughter of the southern Sidhe king Bodbh Dearg, who had been turned to the dangers of a wild deer's life for refusing to love the Danann druid Fear Doirche. She'd lived as such for 3 years, in a place of geas-bound secrecy, while he tried to make her accept him. A servant of the dark man took pity on her, telling her that if she could gain the hospitality of na Fianna and step foot in their Dún homestead, she would be free of the form of a deer. And so, there she was.

Though there are many great love stories in the Irish tales, you could say that this next bit was one of the sweetest, and you wouldn't be telling a lie. The pair were married, and such was the strength of their desire for each other that all other interests fell away, save their time together and the intoxication, the sheer satisfaction, it gave them both. Fionn saw that he'd just been filling in gaps he didn't even know he'd had, til she showed up.

But sure, the outside world wouldn't be put on hold forever. The Lochlannach, those Scandinavian raiders, were busy at the Hill of the Oaks, and the Fianna needed their leader. For seven days they fought, and won, but returning on the eighth day Fionn was surprised not to see his princess awaiting him as he crossed the valley towards home. It turned to dismay, and devastation, when the servants at the keep told him that Sadbh had been tricked out beyond the walls by what seemed the form of himself and his hounds, and even the sound of his hunting horn. She had joyous news for her husband, she'd said, and though they tried to stop her she rushed forth, only to be met by a dark and empty shadow, and hit with the strike of a hazel wand, which returned her to the form of a deer and seemed to lead her away, despite her obvious reluctance and fear.

To say Fionn searched for her is a drop in the ocean of what that man went through. It seemed he wouldn't rest til every rock in the land was turned over to try and find her. For years he looked, and found nothing, no trace... until the day his hounds found a wild boy in the woods, whose face reminded him of his lost love, and whose age seemed to match the time she'd been away from his arms.

Unsure as yet, he took the boy in and began to teach him the ways of human folk, and as the boy learned to speak he told strange tales... but sure, they are all stories for another day.

32

Fionn's Feast

When Fionn MacCumhaill summoned his warriors for a feast, all came – for a gathering given by Fionn was a gathering not to be missed. And so he did, one day, and so they came to his feast.

Every man of them, and his clann, arrived to the great hall at Tara on the appointed day. Fionn sat in the Chief Captain's chair, in the centre, with Goll Mac Morna set in front of him, and every man and woman of them set out in their rightful place. There was Fionn's son Oisín, and his grandson Oscar, Diarmuid (they say his face was lovely and gay, in the old stories, but I don't think that means what you might think it means), and Caelte Mac Ronan, Fionn's brother Caireall White Skin, and Goll's brother Conan the Swearer. Indeed, there were too many to name; they all had their runners and their Poets along, and the whole hall bristled with the banners of war and battle torches of the Gael that each clann carried when visiting.

Each person there was served food to delight the desires, right to the bursting point of their bellies, and then the golden, bejewelled drinking horns were passed around; they were full of sweet, smooth stuff, and none of that moonshine muck, I can tell you. Goll looked at Fionn, and Fionn looked at Goll, and the two of them spread such satisfied smiles that you'd think nothing could wipe them off at all. Music hushed as the Poets stepped forward, as this was their time to shine at any great gathering. It was also their time to get paid, for when the assembled clans were happy with their declamations, gifts were bestowed and they could go home with full pockets as well as full bellies, and sure what Poet wouldn't want that?

Fergus True-Lips began, and he sang the deeds of Fionn and his ancestors, great and mighty. When he was finished, finally, Fionn's family weighed him down with costly presents, until even he - who was well used to the benevolence of good men – was astonished and delighted with the tribute. Goll Mac Morna, with his generosity well oiled by fine liquor, realised that he wouldn't be able to match that standard with what he had about his person, and so he summoned his runner for a word. He asked her, who was near the swiftest and strongest among them, if she had collected the tribute due him from the King of Denmark and Norway. She had indeed, and was able to triple again Goll's supply of treasure, and leave him well assured that he'd not be shown up as niggardly at this nice gathering of friends and family. Whatever Fionn had given Fergus was doubled again by Goll Mac Morna, to the surprise of all there, and the mild annoyance of Fionn himself.

It wasn't really the done thing to outshine your Chief like that, but as the Poets progressed, and Goll oiled that generosity more and more liberally, his gift-giving prowess was growing at about a steady pace with Fionn's irritation, and the discomfort of all around him. Eventually, the Fianna Leader queried his second in command, as to where and how he came across such tribute from the King across the Northern seas. Goll, always keen to share a story he loved, regaled the hall with his tale of travels to the land of Saxons, and battle with Fionn's own father. It was only when he remembered it was that very same battle at which Fionn's father had been killed, by him, that it started to dawn on him that this might not be the best place to be telling that tale. Fionn closed his eyes, took a deep breath, and tried to salvage the situation by reminding Goll that he had a hundred men to every one of his, and perhaps that should be an end to it. Goll's response – "Well, so had your father" – put an end to the pretense of calm, and started a riot and a court case that is still sung of.

But sure, they are all stories for another day.

33

The Red Haired Hare

The oak door boomed, with a fierce thumping that shook the drying bundles of herbs right out of the rafters across the great hall. The Chief, sitting up at the top table, plucked a bit of dried nettle that had fallen into his cup, and – as puzzled as the rest of them about who could be making such a racket outside on that wild night – he gestured for the beams to be lifted and the door thrown open.

The gale from outside billowed in, throwing rain and twigs across the floor, and lifting the food off the plates of those who sat the closest. She stood on the threshold, with a cloak of dirty red wrapped tight around her, hood up against the storm though it fought her every step to tear it down and away off into the night. She didn't wait to be asked, but made her way inside with what would, ordinarily, have been a purposeful stride, but now was hindered and hobbled by an obvious injury to her left thigh. Once in, she threw off the hood, shaking loose the red head of curls for which she was well known, even then, and saying not a word til she stood right in front of the top table, and looked the Chief square in the eye.

"You owe me an honour price", says she, "for the damage was done to me when your hounds were ahunting today in my woods." The Chief knew well there'd been no damage done to her, nor any person, that day, for the Gilly was well trained to tell all on his return from any hunt. All he'd reported was a hare run down near the end of the day, though it'd gotten away before the kill, more's the pity. He also knew those woods were no more hers than they belonged to his Gilly, but her family had the cottage by there for generations now, and the local stories went that they weren't the type of folk that'd be wise to mess with (and whatever it was that had the neighbours afeared seemed to be growing stronger with each passing generation) so the Chief left well enough alone on that one. He asked her what she thought the honour price was owed for, and didn't she bare her own thigh right there and then; the creamy white of it slashed through with a big mouthed bite that could only have come from one of the Chief's own hounds indeed, for other dogs weren't the size of them, and all the wolves had been hunted out long since.

She turned to the Master of the Hound, and asked him straight out if that bite, fresh as it was, could only have come from one of the Chief's hounds, and he had to agree there was nothing else local that could have made it so fresh and so obvious. When the Chief refused to credit it, saying he knew the only thing they had run down that day was a fine puss of a hare, her nod and stony stare was all it took to draw the breath from every person in the place in shock.

But what could he do? Paying her would only show him believing in the magic long since thought to have been stamped from the land. He shook his head, and bid her leave, though the poisonous words then spewing from her mouth were enough to pale the staunchest noble at his tables. Her curse on his hounds just riled his temper even further, so he rose himself and pulled her off out into the night, with her cursing still heard after the stout beam was wrested back in place to bar the door.

She stayed there, just outside the hall, right through that night. Only at dawn, when she heard the first wails and cries as they found the stiff, cold forms outside in the kennels, did she pick up her skirts and begin the walk back to her cottage, where she lived for many a year more, with many more wails and cries on account of her... but sure, they are all stories for another day.

34

The Hearth in the Hall

He jumped the fire one final time, and then he was done with the hearth of Fionn.

Gathering his belongings took little time, and because he'd been banished, he got to take it all. He left the hearth, left the hall, and went out on the ways where none could follow, for those in the household had lost the art of weaving between worlds this long time.

Most of them at least.

When all had settled again, and the men had gone back to drinking to unshake themselves after seeing their leader in such a state, one of the Dési girls that had been taken with me from Dún Iascaig - and she was a girl, a mere youngling who had no business, but no choice, being in this company and so far from home - she came and she sat near me, by the women's fire at the end of the hall.

Usually, the light was better down here, but the dusk had drawn in fast and low, and we sat in deep shadow that suited my mood. Speaking soft, so only my ears caught up to it, she says: "Do you miss home, Lady?"

Home. That was not my home girl, though you were too young to remember my arrival there now. They took me first from another place altogether, and I stayed a while at Femen, with the Sidhe-knoll there so tantalisingly close... before they moved my anchor stone to Dún Iascaig, and when this Fianna came there to raid they were only glad to give me over, stone an all, and move me on again.

And when they brought me here, Fionn knew what I am. Of course he did sure.

He took it to himself to woo me, though he must have known it would never work. I am not for the likes of him, grand hero an all that he styles himself to be, even with the added insight he carries accidentally in that thumb. But he's a stubborn lad, I'll give him that. He didn't give up.

When I saw the other though, here in the hall...

As the food cooked on the hearth, changing and reforming within the fires, this one, he leapt over it, and back. Time and again he did the jump over the flames, and as he did it I knew him for one of mine. For the hearth magic is ours, same as it ever was, and here was another of us, here in this world, working and weaving the ways of my people where all could see but none could understand.

Dearg Corra, they called him, the red peaked one.

On account of his flame hair, they told me, but I knew it was for the fires. And I knew I wanted him for mine, as I'd be his. For to be together in this place wouldn't be quite so bad, as to be alone.

It was hard now, to get time unobserved to speak to one who was ostensibly a servant there, and I a woman who had the attention of the Chieftain. But I finagled my way out to see him, and I carried with me my anchor stone - the magic didn't draw from me as long as I stayed within the boundaries of the hall - so that he would know me for one from his place, as I knew him for one from mine.

The conversation didn't go as I wanted though. He showed me his anchor, well enough, a bowl of pure white bronze, and didn't he seem quite taken with it, prison though it was to one of our kind?

"You carry love for Fionn!", says I, surprised as I realised it to be true.

And he wouldn't have me on account of it, not even to sweeten the bond in order to better work together to free these forms from the anchors. He liked it there, says he to me, and was happy enough to stay and tend hearth for Na Fianna, and for Fionn.

Well, I fair lost my head I must admit.

It was the last thing in this world I had been expecting to hear from out of his mouth, and sure nothing could prepare you for that sort of a shock. I shouted and raged, and the sparks flew. I'd say the fires all over the hall grew brighter, fuelled by the anger of one of us... and it was enough to prick the curiosity of Fionn. Then sure, didn't he stick his blasted thumb in his gob and it led him straight to us? We were found, and he was furious.

He knew well now that nothing had happened, for he didn't find us entwined but weren't we facing off instead? It didn't matter though, not to him and his pride. Me, he kept closer. But Dearg Corra was banished on some pretence of a charge.

'Go hence,' says he, 'out of my sight, and thou shalt have a truce of three days and three nights, and after that beware of me!'

As if he could harm one of us, beyond the cruel bondage in which we were being kept.

The poor crathure who'd only tried to stay loyal, despite all that had been done to him... He jumped the fire one final time, and then he was done with the hearth of Fionn. He took his own anchor bowl, released from the bond, and away then to the forest he went.

Now, that's not the last time he and the bould Fionn MacCumhaill met – in this world or the other – but sure, they're all stories for another day.

35

The Fairy Lover

The fire crackled and hissed, as life escaped from sticks and seeped from turf that had lain long idle in watery bogs. Each new noise made him jump a little, each spark that fell seemed fascinating to a mind that hungered to focus on something, attend to anything but the blank white page before him.

There was no sound from outside the cottage though, at this hour even the night creatures usually heard shuffling along on their business were abed. He had sat through the long, empty darkness all alone, again, since he had banished her from the house. He couldn't have accepted what she had to offer. The price was too high, the cost too great to bear. Many had warned him through long years of training, of the possibility that she might appear. Or one like her, for there were many who sought the likes of him in this land, many who would pull and call and tempt and offer the worlds to a poet's soul. His Masters had gone through it with each apprentice, and when it came his time to teach he had issued the same dire warnings, extolled the same ghastly consequences.

Out of the mounds they came, the Leanán Sidhe. Fairy Lovers: bright was their light, their gifts, their love. Strong burned the creative fires that they stoked and tended in a poet's soul; his musical, magical, poetic inspiration, but with the gifts were balanced the ties that bind, for once a Fairy Lover gained entry to a man's body and soul, she did not ever give them back. Their love was a deadly delight.

She had come to him first on a night just like this. A fire burning in the hearth of his small cottage on the hillside, a long and lonely night awash in the void of mundanity, with not a trickle or a spark of creative inspiration to be found. The gentle tap tap tapping on a window, thought at first to be a branch or twig, but persistent enough to breach the miasma surrounding his heavy head. When he opened the door, she stood a little out of the light that spilled into the night, back from the threshold, and she spoke to him quickly, offering all the things they had said she would, in a voice as soft as the velvet nub on a new calf's horns. He listened, and was tempted, and resisted; refusing to invite her inside, refusing to accept the offers... but knowing that his refusal bound her to him as surely as he would be bound to her if he had accepted.

That was three moons ago now, and she had never left.

Constantly calling, she haunted his dreams, and shadowed the windows of his house as she circled each night. Her voice came to him awake or asleep, whispering dreams when he had no defences, tapping at his attention when he would try and concentrate, or create. Useless, pointless exercises that served no purpose other than to frustrate him. She stayed beyond his reach, impossible to banish, although the Rowan and cold iron charm his old Master had recommended for the threshold served the purpose of ensuring that she could not cross, no matter the weakened state she found him in. He was safe inside.

As he stared again at the plain white sheet that signalled his failure, his lack of resource, he realised that he'd had enough. In a dream, he rose from the table in the centre of his room, and walked to pull open the door. Reaching up, he ripped the charm from the lintel, raised his arm, and threw his protection out into the blackness beyond. Then he waited.

When she came, it was with a sigh of silk that instantly calmed his mind and balmed his spirit. His eyes drank her beauty, as she touched his flesh and entered his home. She would drink of his love, and give in return, and his pages would fill with bounty... until she took all that he was. That wasn't the first or last of the Sidhe ever to take a man... but sure, they are all stories for another day.

36

The Hurling Hero

Fionn MacCumhaill had lost a wife, and found himself unable to have slumber or sweet sleep, he said, without a fitting woman in his bed. Diorruing, a Druid of the Fianna, he said to him that he knew a woman who would be a fitting wife, and then some.

And he found himself sent, in secret, to the house of Cormac son of Art, and king at Tara – to seek the hand of his daughter Gráinne there, the woman that was fairest of feature and form and speech of all the women of the world together, and so they said. Cormac couldn't say yay or nay to the request though, for Gráinne had refused every man and sundry who came before, but she seemed well disposed to the offer from Fionn, and proposed a feast for them to meet and promise.

What they didn't know, these men who would seal her fate, was that she had already chosen the man she'd marry, for one day before when there was a muster and a gathering on the plain of Tara, Fionn and the seven battalions of the standing fian were there that day; and there arose a great hurling match between two kings, with the stout champions of Tara arisen on one side, and the Fianna of Erin on the other. It happened that the game was going against the Fianna, until a one of the fian stood up, and took the hurl off another man, and won the goal three times on the warriors at Tara. She found out after that this was Diarmuid, the grandson of Duibhne the white-toothed, of the lightsome countenance; that is, the best lover of women and of maidens that was in the whole world, and so they said.

So she accepted the plans that were made around her, and all the while she made her own. When the whole court sat around her to feast, on the appointed night, she sent her handmaid for the jewelled golden-chased goblet that had been a gift from a Druid who was her foster sister. When it was filled it held the drink of nine times nine men. Her handmaiden passed it round, and in its wake was laid a trail of trance and sleeping stupor, but not upon Diarmuid and those friends sat around by him.

Gráinne rose and went down to the lads who were yet awake, and she repeated aloud her thoughts of the evening: ""I marvel at Fionn MacCumhaill that he should seek such a wife as I, for it were fitter for him to give me my own equal to marry than a man older than my father."

"Say not that, O Gráinne," said Oisín, son of Fionn, "for if Fionn were to hear thee he would not have thee, neither would I dare to take thee." And with that road neatly closed to her she turned to Diarmuid, and asked him for courtship. He refused, lovely as she was, and so: "Then," said Gráinne, "I put thee under a geis of danger and of destruction, O Diarmuid, that is, under the taboos of mighty druidism, if thou take me not with thee out of this household tonight, ere Finn and the king of Erin arise out of that sleep." She told him of the hurling match too; "I turned the light of mine eyes and of my sight upon thee that day, and I never gave that love to any other man from that time to this, and will not forever."

Well now, Diarmuid asked his comrades what he should do there and then, but sure they were all a bit stumped to be honest, and of the mind that there was nothing really he could do but be bound by the geis and take her away out of there. He countered though, and said he wouldn't take her if she appeared to him by day or by night, clothed or unclothed, on foot or on horseback, in company or without company. And she goes away off the next day, to a sidhe woman who gives her clothing made of mountain down. When she shows up to him at dusk, clad in misty down, and on the back of a he-goat (who everyone knows is no company at all)... Diarmuid has no choice then but to take her away with him.

There's many a tale more to be told about Diarmuid and Gráinne, as they flee and fly from Fionn of the Fianna... but sure, they are all stories for another day.

37

The Mothers

The fire crackled and spat sparks to the deepening sky.

Oisín poked it sullenly with a green willow stick, then turned his head to scan the horizon, again, above the hollow in which they sat - waiting for his friends' arrival.

"Where are they at, at all? We'll have to stay the night here now, and move on at first light in the morning. We told them we wanted to be there at dawn, not only leaving this place by then... sure they said they'd meet us here an' all by the afternoon!"

Fionn, on the other side of the fire from his son, stayed silent. It was true they'd have to stay the night now, and their plans were askew. But without the impatience of youth spurring him, the older warrior tended to take the opportunity to relax where it presented itself. Even unexpectedly.

He hoped nothing had happened to the twins though. He was awful fond of them.

After a while, Oisín went to get more wood. The store they'd gathered on arrival had dwindled, on account of them not expecting to be staying on this long. His father sat and looked into the fire, his mind playing over the possible reasons for the twins' delay this day. Though this wasn't an essential part of their training – more of an entertaining experience for the youngsters – they were usually on time.

He'd gone past wondering, to worried, but hadn't quite reached the point where he'd put his thumb in his mouth to gain the knowledge of it, when he heard the sound of raised voices over the horizon. Rising to his feet immediately, senses alert, his hand was at his weapon before conscious thought caught up with him, and he realised the sound he was hearing was bickering young warriors, as Oisín and the twins made their way back to the campfire, each of them carrying an armload of wood. When they were done stacking and grading the wood, they settled themselves around and he greeted them each with a nod.

"Broccan. Corre. I hope you're well?"

"Aye we are Fionn", said Corre, the elder (by three minutes), "and we're sorry to have kept you late. It couldn't be helped."

"It was the fault of our mother", pitched in Broccan, "she had a pile of chores for us to do, and would hear none of it about our responsibilities to you!"

Watching the scowls, Fionn knew the depth of their frustration, but kept his whist as Oisín commiserated with them on the unfairness of the situation. The boy didn't remember much of his own mother, though her memory was strong with Fionn still, and would remain so. When they'd passed an hour or more of his silence and their harping about their poor mother though, he'd had quite enough.

"So ye think the demands of one mother is a lot to be dealing with, do ye? Try growing up with three!"

"Three mothers Fionn? Sure how did ya end up with three mothers at all?" That was Broccan, speaking for them both, for her sister looked pure stunned to silence with the horror of the thought altogether.

Oisín of course knew the stories of the women well, so Fionn wasn't surprised as he stayed silent and tended the fire, while his father told the tale.

He told them of his birth mother of course, Muirne, who had been pregnant when his father was killed by Goll. She had a beautiful neck, so she did, and many suitors. Her father was a druid who had foreseen the loss of his home should she marry though, and was having none of that – until the bould Cumhal came and took her away. When her son was born, she knew the danger he was in, and so gave him to be raised in secret in the forests of the Slieve Bloom mountains.

Those doing the raising of him then were his father's sister, the druid Bodhmall, and her lifelong companion, the warrior Liath Luachra. From these women he learned to hunt, to kill, to do magic, and to survive, though his father's enemies continued to seek for him. They kept him safe, but there was always a warning word and work to be done from one or the other – or both - so don't be worrying too much about the demands of your own one mother, said he to the twins.

Noticing the firewood stack had gone low again, Oisín raised himself to go fetch more. Before he left the circle of light though, he paused and looked each of them in the eye.

"I dunno what you're all giving out about your mothers for, at all – sure mine was a deer my whole life," said he, as he turned and walked into the darkness.

And there's more could be told of Oisín's tale... but sure, they are all stories for another day.

IV

The Cycle of Kings and Queens

38

About This Time...

This is a quare oul grouping now, because though it starts with recorded history, and when we began writing things down as they happened - ostensibly - it stretches out a long while beyond that, and in either direction I'd say, to be honest.

They call it the Cycle of Kings, and I add in the Queens myself because, well, there's a few of them too, and other mighty women I'd not like to be the one to be disregarding or disrespecting.

And sometimes it's named the Historical Cycle, on account of it supposedly being the 'proper' written history. But sure we all know the monks and scribes would be putting their own spin on things on occasion, adding in bits about the bible and such, and trying to make it all fit with their new world view. And in fairness, at times they just wouldn't be understanding what was going on, the Gaelic culture has strong oul roots and they run down deep, and if the new boys had no context for that... well.

We can't blame them for getting things tangled and a bit confused on occasion, can we?

This whole cycle has been categorised as a fine mix of genuine history with symbolic fiction, so I've included all the stuff in here that can, and does, run right on through to modern Ireland and the stories we still tell.

One thing is for sure, and this applies I believe to all of the story cycles, and to be honest is not something you'll see too much of in my own retellings - our Irish lore has suffered more than nearly any other culture from the determined euphemerisation of deities, that is, treating the old Gods as human rather than divine.

Our Pagan past is so strong, and so solidly rooted in the land and her people, that it formed (and still does, thankfully) a very real threat to an invasive and eventually conquering religious ideology.

The Old Gods were written as human, and the old ways dismissed as 'the illusions of demons'; quite literally, for in the margins of one of our texts we see one grumpy scribe write in Latin...

> *"But I who have copied this historia or, more accurately, fabula, do not give credence to certain things in this historia or fabula. For certain things in it are the illusions of demons; certain are poetic fictions; certain are plausible, certain are not; certain are for the entertainment of fools".*
> *- the Book of Leinster (LL) text of the Táin Bó Cúailnge. Translated by Best and O'Brien.*

As I said though, it's not something you've to worry about me doing in this book, or my other stories. The Old Gods have made themselves felt, and very present and undeniable, in my own life, and that of those around me.

So I personally believe the stories of the ancients, when they tell us of myth and magic interweaving between the worlds, of a parallel existence, interchange, and learning between this world and the Other.

Take it as you will, Dear Reader, for there's nobody here going to tell you that you have to believe it too.

ABOUT THIS TIME...

But do know that the Tales of Old Ireland, at least, are alive and well, and being retold in the land, by her people, as we cycle through the stories once more.

39

A Wolf Story

It is said, that in the time of Britain's Queen Elizabeth - when the English troops made endless war against the Irish – there were more wolves in Ireland than there were men.

A certain farmer out in Connacht, by the name of Connor, got up one morning to find his two best breeding cows had been taken in the night, with no sight nor sound of them when he walked his fields. He suspected wolves, and indeed, didn't he pick up a track of them on the edge of his land, and set off following; with only a thick blackthorn stick in hand for protection, as the Irish were forbidden at the time to carry any true weapons.

By and by, he came upon a low hut, half covered over like the den of a robber or a wild animal. The wolf trail led right to the door, and Connor, being both brave and a little stupid, strode right up to it and started banging. It was answered by a thin old man, stooped and grey, but with fierce black eyes that took the measure of Connor then and there. He invited the lad inside, to meet his wife, who sat curled by the fire, just as thin and old and grey and wily as her husband seemed. When she smiled at Connor, he saw there was no sign of old age on the teeth in her head; which looked awful strong, and gleamed slightly in the light filtering inside.

They bade him sit by the hearth, but he'd barely been settled a minute when the door banged open and in loped a young wolf with an ink black coat. Connor hadn't time to do more than jump up in alarm before the wolf padded over to the bedroom beyond the parlour and slipped inside. He was back out in no time, but now came as a fine young man, with ink black hair and dressed only in rough trews, so his bare chest could still be seen. He told Connor be still and be seated, for he was standing rigid in shock, clutching his blackthorn stick and eyeing the family warily.

He'd heard of such things as this, of course, but nobody he knew had ever seen it in life. The young wolf man assured him he was in no danger, and this was why. Many years before, a much younger Connor had been walking the woods when he came across a wolf pup, lying by a stream but near dead from thirst, as he couldn't move for the pain of the long thorn stuck in his side. Connor had removed the thorn, cleaned the wound, and stayed with the pup while he drank. Then he'd left him in peace. "Blessings are won by a good deed done", said the wolf man, and so he invited Connor to eat and stay for a drink, and no harm would come to him in their house. Well, one drink turned to many, and by the flickering light of the hearth fire Connor finally lay to rest that night, full drunk in a peaceful slumber.

When he woke the next morning it was to harsh sunlight piercing his eyelids. He sat up carefully - for even his hair felt sore – and found he'd been asleep in his own fields. Picking his way back home, he figured it for a dream maybe, though the hangover assured him there'd been drink taken in reality. Puzzling, he walked right into a cow that shouldn't have been there, one of three such fine creatures, who stood in his usually empty garden. Figuring them for wanderers from a neighbours field, he tried to shoo them out – but they were met by the snapping teeth of a lone black wolf outside in the lane, and quickly decided that the front garden was the very place for them to be. Connor eyed the wolf, and the wolf eyed Connor, and with a small nod each for the balance restored, they both turned for home.

He never could find that hut again, though that wasn't the last we'll hear tell of wolves.

But sure, they are all stories for another day.

40

The Crop Haired Girl

She couldn't stop jigging. Peig was trying to brush out her hair, had been trying for a good while now, if truth be told, but every move or noise outside had young Grace turning and twisting, making more tangles in the long brown tresses. With comb and bristle she was trying to tame the curly mane, but sure it was as wild as the head on which it grew, and the mouth that lived under it. Arra she may as well be trying to plait the scrubby gorse on the hillside above, for all the taming that she could achieve.

A clatter in the courtyard below had her hopping up, again, and away before the old hands could get a grab of her. Peig was sore tempted to just give up and let her run off with that tangled bush atop her skull, but her mother'd be having kittens at seeing her like that, again, and especially on a day that Dubhdara was due home, and away again right after. Sure the poor man would hardly get time for a dinner before he'd be setting off for Spain on the evening tide. The child at the window caught a glimpse somehow through the narrow arrow slit of what she was waiting for, and she hared out across the room before old Peig had even a chance to catch a hold of her. Dragging back the great oak door, she was out and away, followed only by the dismayed wail of her nursemaid, and with her still tangled mane streaming out behind her. Somewhere down the hallway, the useless comb dislodged itself and dropped to the flagstone floor in her wake.

She was fast as the wind, but still by the time she scooted down all the steps and corridors of her father's castle, the men were already inside in the hall with the doors shut. Shane Mór stood guard outside, and he pretended not to know her when she fetched up in front of him, out of breath and outraged to be kept from her Daddy here at the last hurdle. He wouldn't let her through until she delivered him a swift kick in the shins for his messing. Laughing and hopping, he opened the doors so she could barrel across the hall and begin asking her father if she could go to Spain with him. Surely this time she'd be let. She knew her way well around the ships, and all the skills she'd need, and it was well past time for her first long journey.

Margaret O'Malley was aghast at seeing the little harpy that hurled itself through the hall to land at the feet of her husband and begin to pester for a sea voyage. That hair! Sure she couldn't do a thing to make a noble lady of her only daughter, but she had to keep trying and that was that.

Scooping the girl up, she ignored the threshing and screaming, and apologised to her husband. She carried Grace off, scolding her that girls did not go to sea, not ever, and she'd to go right back to Peig to get her hair dressed and fit for polite company. She returned to the hall and she scolded her husband too, for indulging the girl and playing on with her flights of fancy. A girl at sea indeed – sure where did they think they were going with that one?

Dinner was served up and the men fell to eating, talk moved forwards and plans were being made for the Spanish trip. Then the doors opened again and Shane Mór walked through, and sure they knew something was up because he was supposed to be staying outside, and he couldn't keep a straight face besides. He announced the arrival of a new sailor, a crop haired wee thing who he was sure would do well at sea. In strutted Grace with her hair all shorn off, and well dressed in boy's clothes... to the wails of her long suffering mother.

That was the day that Gráinne Mhaol – 'Bald Grace' – earned her first sea journey, and went on to many adventures as the Pirate Queen of Ireland.

But sure, they are all stories for another day.

41

The Woman in the Castle

"Would ya ever sit down woman? You'll wear a hole in the floor there!"

Gráinne paused mid stride only to cast a withering glare, before continuing her rapid pace over and back through the great hall. How could she sit down? Sure wasn't he due back here any time now, and what would his response be when he found what he'd find here?

It was true to the year and day since she'd married him - Risdeard an Iarainn Bourke, or Iron Richard as the English named him. And not just for the ancestral maille he wore either... ah he was a hard man and no mistake. According to the Old Laws, the marriage was perfectly legitimate. She'd agreed to marry him for one year certain, and that was that.

His land and holdings were attractive, and sure wasn't it a fine time they'd had together besides all that? The child she now bore was a bonus, for the sport they'd enjoyed in the meantime was the main reason that man had pursued her for so long. And he seemed to enjoy what was between her ears as much as what was between her legs... it was a shame to treat him so now, for he'd surely see it as a betrayal. But no. No matter all that. She must do what must be done.

Running her hands through close cropped hair, Gráinne went to stand by the blazing fire. The hall was alive with the comings and goings of her people. She'd gathered all she could to Carraigahowley Castle, all that weren't at sea on business, or tending their own business on land. 'Rockfleet' they called it, standing proud by the port, and holding much other land and useful sheltered harbours where many a great ship could be anchored discreetly, with none the wiser for it.

The doors banged back, and a runner stood panting and clutching his side. "They're here Gráinne, he's coming up over the rise now."

She whirled into action, barking orders for men to move and the castle to be secured before he approached. When all was done to her satisfaction, she climbed the tower stairs to the hall above, where she could watch from the top window as he made his way to the gates.

Ah, but he was a handsome man still. Tall, and broad of shoulder, with a strength and wit to match her own, it was a pure shame to be done with him so soon. He sat the saddle of his horse below her, facing the locked castle gates, and speaking quietly with his Second, who had pulled up alongside him. After a while had passed, and some furious knocking had been undertaken by his party and largely ignored by hers, he pulled back a ways and looked up. His grey eyes met Gráinne's, and they shared a mutual acknowledgement, for at this point he must surely have known exactly what she was about.

His voice startled her, calling through the silent evening. "You've locked me out of my own castle Gráinne stór, will ya not let me in so I can get some supper and share the warmth of our fires?"

"I will not be letting you in again Risdeard, as well you know... our year is done and there'll be no more sharing the fires for you and I in this lifetime. I'll keep our child safe and warm behind these walls though, and you can be pleased about that, at least."

"Right pleased I'd be, if we could rear that babe together with this castle as our home. Sure let me in a grá, and we'll talk about it inside."

"I married you for one year certain, and there's none of that year left to us now. Be gone from the castle I hold and keep, and the lands that surround it, Risdeard an Iarainn Bourke, I dismiss you!"

Hearing the formal words from her lips, Iron Richard ruefully shook his head, and gave the command to turn and go from the property, for they were now divorced by the laws of the land.

That's not the last we'll hear of the bould Gráinne Mhaol, Sea Queen of Ireland, sitting in her keep at Rockfleet.

But sure, they are all stories for another day.

42

Grace and Elizabeth

When her men start to grumble at the long wait, and Shane Mór makes a comment under his breath about the length of time it takes an English Queen to powder her behind to greet folk - Gráinne laughs right along with them.

Standing together outside the double doors of a great hall, she won't let them see that she's as nervous as a scalded cat before she gets in to see Elizabeth. They've come this far, across the seas and straight up the Thames, and she won't put her clann to shame by showing the English anything other than the fierce pride and strength the O'Malleys are well known for.

This summer palace at Greenwich is far removed from the dirty mess of London, where the plague now stalks streets and alleys, taking down all before it. Here the walls are clean and bright, the people washed and well, and the royal court sleep sound in their beds; while common folk who are attacked by the silent killer in the morning would be dead by nightfall. But it wasn't plague talk that Gráinne would be met with when she finally gained entry to the throne room.

A woman of her own age was within, whose stories well matched her own for strength and pride - and who would have thought that either of them would ever hold such power or live to such an age as sixty long years, with living and working in a man's world? She had to convince this woman, this Queen from across the waves, to instruct the English general, Richard Bingham, to release the O'Malley brother and sons.

As the doors swing open, at last, Gráinne settles herself to walk formally in the tight bodice and wide skirts, far from the breaches she usually dons at sea, for comfort and convenience. All eyes are on her as she enters, but it is the guard who searches her person that is sweating under the glare of Gráinne and her men. His nervousness deepens when he discovers the dagger she concealed, but when he hands it to his officer and reports to the Queen sitting down the hall, she merely beckons Gráinne forward with an impatient wave.

Elizabeth asks a question in English, which Gráinne had never taken to learning – believing it to be a base tongue with no pleasure for the ears on hearing it spoken or sung. Frustrated before she even begins, Gráinne tries a greeting in the scholar's tongue - for surely an English noble will be educated enough to speak it? With slight surprise, quickly masked, Elizabeth repeats her initial question in Latin, allowing a small smile when it was clear the Gael understands her.

"Why the dagger Grace O'Malley? Surely you don't mean to attack the hand of respect as it is extended?"

"No Ma'am" says she, "it is for my own protection only."

Elizabeth nods, unperturbed, and notices then that the woman before her has failed to bend the knee as directed. When she queries this, she receives another calm response in perfect Latin.

"I do not recognise you as my Queen, though I offer respect as a foreign ruler is due," says Gráinne. To this, Elizabeth has nothing to say.

Dust from face powder and treatments for the hair is thick in the air around them, and Gráinne, used to breathing the sea breeze, finds herself irritated to a sneeze. A guard, still standing close, hands her a lace handkerchief provided by a lady-in-waiting... into which Gráinne blows her nose, then turns and throws the sullied scrap on the fire nearby.

Surprised by the gasps and tittering that ensue, but taking her cue from the quizzical expression on Elizabeth's face, Gráinne provides that in Ireland it is deemed uncivilised to keep a used handkerchief about one's person, surely it is better to throw it to burn?

At this, Elizabeth breaks to a genuine smile, and Gráinne knows that the day is half won for it. All that remains is to see to the details at hand, and secure the release of her men folk, which proceeds apace.

This isn't the last we'll hear of the bould Gráinne Mhaol... but sure, they are all stories for another day.

43

The Seven Sisters

In the olden days, people would come, as they do today, to the county of Roscommon for the great hunting and fishing there. A group of just such men were down one day in the woods at Drimnagh, and they spotted a hare there. But even though they fired shot after shot into it, they couldn't bring it down, and followed it instead to a small cottage close by. Here they saw it dash inside, and the door closed tight after it. When they went to follow – their curiosity well piqued I can tell you – they were met by a fierce dog, with fur as black as ink, bleary red rimmed eyes, and a mouth full of curving yellow fangs, who wouldn't let them pass.

They decided the best way to deal with this, and satisfy their own ends, would be to put a shot in the dog too, but every time they tried to do just that, it would snatch the shot out of the air – chomping and crunching as if it was the finest of butcher's bones, until the powder dribbled down his jaws and the barking and snarling resumed. It was not long, with all the noise going on, until a hag came out of the house, and every tooth in her head was as long as the tongs. She had dirty brown hair as tough as wire, and it stuck up out of her head in tangles, like the bushes and briars on a hillside. She asked the travellers what they were doing outside her house, and when they told her they were after a hare they'd shot, a sly smile spread across her face, and she invited them inside to see if they could find it.

Luckily, not all the brave hunters were as clueless as they might have appeared, because one of the boyos stepped forward and asked if there was any other person in the house with her. She said there was indeed: there was her and her six sisters who lived inside in the house in the woods, and she'd get the girls outside to meet them, if they liked. That smile spread again like oil across her face as she whistled for the dog to go inside, and shouted for her sisters to come outside. The first to emerge, after a minute or two, had hair as black as ink, bleary red rimmed eyes, and a mouth full of curving yellow fangs that were just as long as those of the sister they'd seen before her. She also seemed to have a smear of some dark stuff dribbled down her jaws. There wasn't a smile to be seen on her face at all.

The cottage door opened again, and with each fresh sister to face the light outside, the disgust and fear of the hunters grew in force. Maybe 'fresh' is the wrong word to be using for these particular specimens of hag-hood: any one of them would chill the bones of any sane and sensible person just by glancing in your general direction. One sister's body was covered in all manner of hair and bristle and fluff, so she looked part animal altogether. Another had a spiked nail on the end of each finger, as hard as a horn and sharp as a briar. Yet another had a neck all scrawny and long, and she seemed to be able to turn it right round like a chicken. Each of them had a look about them so awful that when you caught sight of her the first time, you never wanted to see her again, and if you had to see her a second time, you thought you might die of fright. It was the last one though, that finally convinced the hunter boys that it was really time to go - for when she appeared in the doorway, they saw her ears had wads of fur sticking out, and she limped toward them, favouring her thigh and cradling her arm. Just as if she'd been shot.

That's not the last we ever heard of the seven sisters in the wood, but sure, they are all stories for another day.

44

Padraig and the Púca

There was a young man in Clare, a miller's son, whose name was Padraig. He worked hard for his father, for they hadn't much, but every day he went to the mill he would have to shout and shuffle the lazy labourers out there to get them to do even a tap of work.

One of the days, when they had a big order on, he couldn't even get them to raise a toe, never mind a finger, and when he went to check at end of day, didn't he find them all fast asleep – and not a bit of the corn was ground for the order.

Frustrated and furious, he walked out along the stream for a bit, and was sitting head in hands when he heard a fierce snorting behind him. Turning, he met a large black bull, pawing the ground and about to charge. Now, Padraig knew there was no such bull with his family nor with the neighbours, and his own mother was a fairy woman, who'd been telling him old tales since he was born – so he could well recognise a Púca no matter what form it was taking. He stood and said that if the Púca would help his family that night, he'd give him his own thick coat to wear, for it was fierce cold. He laid the coat over the shoulders of the bull, and it rested down meek as a lamb, then lumbered off back up to the mill.

Padraig sat for a while by the stream, his head much quieter, and waited, for the fairies don't like to be disturbed in their work. After a time, he saw an old man leave, away into the scrubland behind. The poor thing was skin and bones, and cold even with the heavy coat draped over him, for he was dressed only in rags beneath. When Padraig went into the mill though, he saw the corn all ground; a week's work had been done in a single night and it certainly wasn't the labourers who'd done it, for they were still snoring.

The next night, Padraig was back by the mill at the same time, with a drop of whiskey and a bit of a cake his mam had made, and left them by the door. Sure enough, it wasn't long before he heard the mill working away, and he knew again it wasn't the labourers, for they were all still down at the pub. He went and dismissed the lot of them, and was back in time to see the Púca leave the same as the last night.

This happened every night, and the family grew very rich, for the miller was getting a week's work done in a night, and he never had to pay a wage other than the whiskey and a bit of cake of an evening. But Padraig grew tired of seeing the Púca heading off through all kinds of weather with not even a shoe on his foot, nor trousers to keep his skinny old legs a bit warm. So he got a superb suit of clothes made up, and left them out one night in place of the usual whiskey and cake.

He watched the Púca find them, try them on, and preen as he examined himself looking like a fine gentleman. Indeed, he must have thought himself such, and fine gentlemen don't labour each night in a mill, so he took himself off to see the countryside, and laboured no more. But Padraig didn't mind, for they were wealthy by then, and sold the mill for good profit. He made a match after with a Lord's daughter, and had a fine wedding party with all the trimmings.

At the feast, he found a grand golden cup laid up at the top table, and knew it to be a gift from the Púca, so he insisted that only himself and his bride drink from it that day, and every day thereafter.

The couple never had a day's bad luck in their lives from then on, and their descendants went to many adventures with the fairies. But sure, they are all stories for another day.

45

The Witch of Kilkenny

The footsteps are unhurried, punctuated by a steady drip from dank stone along the corridor.

But they come for her.

Her cell door thumps open. Rough hands grab and lift her. Even the stark wan sunlight of an October dawn hurts her eyes now, but the wind is glorious after stale fetid air, so she turns her face toward it as they lead her across rough cobblestones to the court house, hungering for the feel of the breeze nipping her nose and stirring through her matted hair.

"You are Petronilla, formerly of Meath, recently handmaid servant to Dame Alice Kyteler, she who has since absconded to England and left you to your fate?"

Her eyes take in the bloated smug face of him, Richard De Ledrede, sitting up there gloating at her like the king o' Kilkenny, if there was such a thing... and she spits on the stone floor between them. The Bishop only smiles, and continues.

"You are indeed Petronilla of Meath, and this court will hear your confession, taken nigh 3 days ago in your prison."

Her nostrils flare at that, but she keeps her whist as best she can, knowing full well the court don't care that her 'confession' was taken at the back end of a bullwhip. They said she'd be flogged six times, but it was six times that, or sixty, she don't know and it don't matter neither. She's done for already, an' that's that. His voice grates through her as he carries on.

"The confession stands as such. Petronilla of Meath was immersed and complicit in the foul witchcraft of Dame Alice Kyteler, and the group of heretical sorcerers which surrounded her, up to such date as the Church intervention began, namely the Inquisition led by my holy self, the Bishop of Ossory, in this year of our Lord 1324, with the support of seven nobles of verified Anglo-Norman purity, and five honoured Knights of the Crown.

Specific acts of heresy and witchcraft accorded to Petronilla of Meath are thus: Denial of Faith of the good and holy Roman Catholic Church; blood sacrifice to one Robin, son of Art, an incubus who appeared in various forms, such as a large black cat, a black dog of unnatural size, or a giant dark skinned man in company with two others even more monstrous in form; acting as a Mediatrix between Dame Alice Kyteler, and this Robin; the causing of women of her acquaintance to appear as they had grown the horns of a goat atop their very own heads; the consultation of Demons, and relaying of their responses to the aforesaid group."

He peers down at her from amid his robes of office, from behind his legal palisade, and she seethes to be regarded so by one such as him.

"Do you have anything to say in your defence, foul Witch?"

Did she have anything to say to this court of a law she don't recognise, to these people she had been forced to smile among for so many years? Aye, an' that she did.

"There's one who still walks free among you, who wore the Divil's girdle about his form for the year and day, the very son of the sorceress ye so decry, to whom all her wealth and knowledge was ever bestowed.

I name him William Outlawe, and state freely that his fate should match my own, for his deeds ever did.

And I tell ye now, without even the whip to coax it, for I've been left alone to dangle in the wind for this; for all I am a mistress of the Black Arts, as ye say it, I am but a candle to the bonfire of the Dame, she from whom I learned all knowledge and skill."

She didn't know it, as she was led from the court, but it wasn't the hanging tree that stood stark in her future. For on Sunday, 3rd of November in 1324, Petronilla was burned alive, the first such instance of death by fire for the crime of heresy on the island of Ireland.

That's not the last we'll hear tell though, of witches in old Éire... but sure, they are all stories for another day.

46

The Hags with the Bags

When the Black Thief of Sloan was in a tight spot, a story told of adventures past would often serve to pave the way clear, or at least distract enough to bring about the means of an escape.

One of the best ran such, and twas clear a favourite as much for the casual recounting of the Thief's fame and renown as for anything else.

"In my youth now, I was a wild one, and would often roam the countryside in search of treasure... or indeed, just an interesting distraction would do. Once in particular, of the many distresses I found meself in, I was benighted away out in the countryside with not a light nor a soul to be seen for miles all round. And sure where would I sleep, I asked meself?

I came upon an oul kiln, so I did, with the ribs of it still solid, and the stones still standing round it giving some shelter to the sides, if not from the sky. I didn't have much in the way of choice, that night, so I settled down in the ribs, and sleep soon took me.

During the depth of it, I heard a rattle and the harsh grating of voices, kept low but coming upon me fast enough – too fast to be gettin meself away anywhere else at least. I stayed settled there, full awake and waiting. Into the stones and bones of the kiln came three oul hags, and it wasn't long before it came clear that they were of the same mind as me, to sleep right there the rest of the night. Their voices were kept low, but didn't I hear them talking about none other than meself! Sayin that they'd to keep a close eye on the heavy gold that each carried in her own bag, for fear the Black Thief would take it from her, quick as you could blink.

Well, what's a thief to do only live up to the reputation that's chasing ya round the countryside? The problem I had was the hags had laid their gnarled and rotting heads on their bags there to sleep, and I had to feel around for some sods of oul turf and swap them out for the gold, before making off out across the fields with the 3 bags of gold, quick as ya like.

I hadn't gone far though before I heard their shrieks running on after me, and I knew for sure and for certain, the chase was on. Not long after that, I spotted a hare, and a hawk, and a hound... all chasing me from back the way I'd come. I figured then the hags had the Sidhe power to shift form, and this might not go well for me if I was caught. I had my broadsword, of course, but sure what use would that be to me if they had the power to come alive again after I had done with them? All in all, I thought it best to try and hide and let them past, for I was fast running out of options and they'd see me clearer with the coming dawn. I climbed a tree, with sword and gold an all tugged up behind me, but sure they were on me like a shot.

Gathered round the base, they formed an odd plan, though effective. One turned to an anvil, one to a lump of ore... and the other crafted a hatchet to bring me down, tree and all. They'd me done for, until the last stroke was about to fall. Didn't the cock crow just then, and dawn broke, and the three hags just disappeared away with the coming of the light!"

Now, the Black Thief of Sloan, the wiliest in all the island at one time, was called such - some would say - for the colour of their cap. Others though, might say the name they gave was for the hair that lay neat under that cap, for those locks were as black as the wing of a crow, flying across a dark moon at Samhain time.

But aren't they only the ones that had met her?

There are many more tales to be told of the Black Thief... but sure, they are all stories for another day.

47

The Spit Milk

The Rourke sisters lived in there, so they did.

That old stone cottage right there, yeah. They had the 2 acres, and the dairy, and you can see the remains of the outhouse there too. See it?

They would have been quite wealthy you know, for the time. But the work was hard, with the cattle an' all. And it was just them sure, in the house there on their own, they'd no man about the place.

Ah don't look at me like that now. That was a thing back in them days, a thing they would have thought they needed most likely - a man to do or help with the harder work - or at least it was a thing that other folk would have been telling them they needed.

So anyway, these two women were living here on Uisneach Hill. Some say they were ould, really getting on in the years, but some others now they say the sisters weren't all that old at all.

One morning, the younger one of 'em went out to the dairy there to milk. As she was milking, didn't a fairy come up to her, and ask her for a noggin of milk. She gave it over straight away, wouldn't you? An' the fairy drank it all down and went away.

The next morning then, when she was out milking again, didn't the very same fairy show up and ask her for another?

THE SPIT MILK

Dutifully, she poured it out straight away, but just before handing it over, she asked what she'd have in return for it.

"Well, what do you want?", says the fairy.

"I'd like... a man about the place for a change," says the sister, "to help with the work an' all that."

"All right so", says the fairy, and takes the noggin of milk she hands over at that.

She watches as the fairy drink it all down, but just as it's finished, didn't the thing spit all the milk right back in her face?

Shocked, so she was, but as she spluttered and groped for a rag or a towel to wipe her eyes, and ended up wiping her whole face on her apron and turning on the fairy with a ferocious glare.

"What in the holy hells did you do that for?"

"You've always been kind to us," says the fairy, "and you never once forgot to give the first few drops from each milking to your Neighbours round here. Not once mind you, and we were always watching!"

The sister shifted uncomfortably round on her milking stool.

"Always watching?"

"Always," says the fairy, definitively. "And do you know what else? You've kept the pathways clear and checked it out before building anything or fencing anything or changing anything... and we do appreciate that, so we do. And your sister inside there is just the same, and your Mammy before ye. So while you live, you'll want for nothing. The Spit Milk is luck to you, and you took it."

With that, the fairy gave her a wink, and told her the wish she'd made would be done, and that she'd be wealthy the rest of her days, before going along on its way.

And do you know what happened?

A young buck showed up, the very next day! Looking for lodging, so he was, and well able to help with the work an' all that, in exchange for a roof above and some food to take under it.

Now, we don't know what else he might have been doing to earn his keep around here, and I suppose now that we never will. But isn't it a grand oul tale all the same?

There's plenty more now that say they've had encounters with the Good Neighbours here on the Hill of Uisneach... but sure, they're all stories for another day.

48

Bear Witness

Limping through the long grass, with the early dew sticking to her skirts, she had to stop on a sharp intake of breath as the pains ripped through her belly again. She staggered on the uneven ground, but kept her feet under her as she put her head down and focused on the lake at the far end of the field she'd crossed into.

That's where the stones are. Brighid will help me now. She's all that can help me now.

The ditches to the side of her were still high after the summer's growth, and there was no-one around this late. They'd all be keeping close to home with the twilight falling and the mists drawing in over the lake as the sun went down.

She clutched the penny in her hand, less shiny now with the sweat and effort she'd had to get both herself and the coin out and away from Mammy this evening. She'd been keeping out of her Mammy's way as much as possible, as it became more and more difficult to hide the belly, to cover herself up so she wouldn't be caught out. Oh God the pure shame of it, even the thought of the look on her poor mother's face if she ever found out what had happened gave her a hot sweat that broke across her skin just as another searing pain rose up inside her, 'til she couldn't tell the shame from the pain... and sure weren't they all the one anyway?

That one did bring her to her knees though, and she stayed there, with the wetness seeping through to her knees, cooling her a little at least while she caught her breath, then forced herself back up to keep going on to the stones. She had to get to the stones.

There was a lot of pain, but she was used to pain now.

The pain of her down there after he'd done what he did to her, telling her all the while how pretty she was and how it wasn't his fault, it was just how God made him. The pain all up inside herself as the thing inside her was growing, for months... moving her own insides round, it felt like, to take up room for itself in her body. The pain of restriction as she wound her belly round in linen strips to try and stop it making her fat, fat like wives got.

That was the pain of trying to stop it from showing to Mammy, who was looking at her more and more these days, it seemed, than she ever had before. The pain in her chest as those things got bigger every day and she had to bind them in linen too. The pain in her back, right down at the bottom, as the weight of the thing inside dragged on her from the front.

This pain was getting worse though. Was it always like this for women? She just made it to the stones as the next one set her on fire, it took her breath and her thoughts and when she could breathe and think again she found there was a wetness between her legs. Had she soaked up water from the moss on the stones... no, it was blood and it was coming from her. Trickling down her legs under her skirts and then there were tears trickling down her face under the sky and she thought that maybe she could cry now, just here. She'd held it in so long and there was only Brighid to see her tears here, for weren't these her stones? And didn't she take care of women and girls who needed her?

Looking at the stones, all laid out and piled up on each other, she saw how they were supposed to work. Turning them sunwise for Brighid's Blessing was the thing they did, to help and to heal. But suddenly – there in the field by the lake, with the wetness leaking from her and the wetness all around her – suddenly she realised that there was no help for her, and no healing to be had.

This was a baby he had put into her. A child. What was he doing giving a baby to her? How could she even raise a child? Why didn't he know that? Why didn't he stop this happening?

This was his fault. She hadn't wanted him to come to her. She hadn't wanted him to touch her, or put things into her. He'd told her it was her fault for being so pretty, and God's fault for making him that way, and everybody's fault but his own.

But it was his. It was his fault.

She put her hands on a stone, the big one in the middle. Struggling to lift it up, she had to stop and rest until after another pain lanced through her, but she got it raised a bit anyway, enough to put her Mammy's penny in under it, and it dropped back with a thunk to the bullaun hollow it sat inside of. It turned easier than it lifted though. She perched on the edge of the stones, with her hand on the big one, feeling how it turned easy this way or that way – deiseal, sunwise, was to help and to heal. But the other way, she'd heard it in whispers. Turning the stone the other way would put a crooked face on a man, and if he deserved it for real it would kill him, her Granny swore it.

Her hand swung the stone in its cradle, to the right, to the left, to the right again. Another pain shot up her spine and down her legs, setting them on fire of agony, and sending a pulse of blood down her legs. Reaching her hand down, she felt the warm thick wetness on her fingers, and then she placed her hand back on the big, beautiful stone as she turned it to the left. Slowly at first, she thought of how he'd given her sweets to keep her quiet. Turning more, and of how he'd come visiting often, to talk to the family he said. But looking at her always. Faster then, she thought of his sweat dripping down on her as he'd done what he'd done. Turning the stone with her bloody hand, her tears dripping down on it as she did what she did. He deserved it. He deserved it for real.

And so it was done.

Spent and needing shelter then, she made her way – slowly, limping, her body full only of pain – back up to where the church was, to shelter within its walls. Behind her was left a trail of her life blood, following the fall of the field, all the way back down to the stones.

That's not the first or the last time the ways of the new religion have put an Irish woman in danger.

But sure, they're all stories for another day.

And another venue, perhaps.

49

The Woman of the House

Mrs. Kennedy (the younger; a name given to her by marriage, though she'd been Ms. Power from birth) wasn't long married all the same, when herself and her husband William got an invite to go live in the big house by Mrs. Kennedy (the elder), after the death of that lady's husband John.

The house was 5 miles out from Ballyduff, in a grand farmland setting, and a sight better than the hovel the young couple were living in, beyond in Lismore, I can tell ya. William was a cousin of the late John Kennedy, and as they'd no children of their own he'd left the house and farm to a nephew, also named John, but with the proviso that they didn't pass on while his wife was still alive and needing a hearth and home for herself.

Well, Mrs. Kennedy (the younger), didn't know herself when they walked up the drive to the big house that first day, it was near enough to May Day, as it happened, and the leaves of the fine crabapple orchard that lined the front were just uncurled, showing their bright fresh green before the promise of heavy blossom. She couldn't help but feel akin to the new life budding in the old trees, with the hope and promise of a fresh start and a good life here, for a while at least, 'til they got on their feet and Mrs. Kennedy (the elder) had no more need for them, in whatever way that came about.

It was a grand house though, with a solid stone wall build and none of that oul mud construct business, and two stories! With a fine wide chimney in the centre that she just knew would hold many a warm family fire beneath. And it did. They moved in and settled, and the years ticked by easily, as time will do. A babby came along for them, and then another; two fine healthy and happy wee ones that she deemed a blessing every day as they grew.

Sure wasn't life just perfect?

Of course now, that sort of stuff never lasts long. We can't have ups without the downs, but Mrs. Kennedy (the younger) hadn't really prepared herself for the inevitable dip that they'd be facing soon enough. Inevitably, the end time of Mrs. Kennedy (the elder) came, and she sickened seriously in a short space of time, old as she was. A sort of low key panic set in, with everyone in the household scrambling around to try and do all they could for her in her time of need. Not that they hadn't been kind enough to her before, but it came very starkly clear to them that the only thing keeping them in their lovely home there was that frail old lady's health - as per the agreement and the Will of John Kennedy (the elder) - and it made them suddenly extra kind indeed.

Nonetheless, she died soon after, and it threw them first into a panic, and then into a slump of depression, in the day of making arrangements for the funeral and burial of the woman of the house. Once they'd put her in the ground, they went back to the house to start the tidy up, and with all the busy-ness of previous days finally done and dusted, William watched his wife finally slump, like a puppet with her strings cut.

"It'll be alright love," says he, though neither of them knew how that could be, with not a penny of savings put away and homelessness looming fast on their horizon.

"Will it now, William? We've nowhere to go!" says she, and watching her leaning over the kitchen table, tears dripping onto the very wood he'd seen her scrub so many times, lay food on to feed the household every day, and sit at with a book or some sewing time after time after time... something snapped in poor William.

"We'll not leave here so," says he. "When the lawyers come, we'll refuse to leave the farm, and make it so we can prove the Will to be false."

"How could it be false?"

"Well, I'm no lawyer myself now, but we'll figure something out. Leave it with me."

He did as he said. When the lawyer arrived the next day to sort the property, he ran him off altogether, then saddled the horse and rode down to Lismore to speak himself to a man who knew about such things, and get advice. The advice he received and the plan he made on the back of it was not, in any way, what you'd call honourable practice. Mostly, it centred on asserting that John Kennedy (the younger), who was due to inherit his uncle's property and had indeed been waiting patiently for a number of years at that point, was a scoundrel who had coerced John Kennedy (the elder) into making the Will as it was. With an added dash of claiming harassment, of both themselves, and the late Mrs Kennedy (the elder). His wife wasn't happy about it at all at all, but William followed it through, determined his family wouldn't end up in a ditch without even a roof above them. It was a strong motivator. They set the lawyers in motion and were informed it would all time quite a while to thrash out, But they could stay in the house til it was sorted. So they settled back in to the family day-to-day and things began to return to normal on the farm.

Within a week though, the dreams began.

Mrs. Kennedy (the younger) was decidedly unsettled in the night-time, often waking her husband with talking, shouts, crying, and thrashing about in the bed. She remembered nothing on waking, she told her husband, but her face began to show the signs of poor sleep, and by the time they'd had a week of that, there was a decidedly haggard look to her, with no signs of improvement.

Then the noises started.

Knocking and kicking were to be heard in the house. Deep, resonant thuds to the front and back door were met with only empty air once the residents went to see who was beyond, looking for access. When the kitchen was empty, they'd often hear a sharp kicking from within, as if someone was angrily lashing out at the walls, the doors, even the legs of the table. Men and women went to the house even in the daytime, nothing could be seen – but all could hear the noises in the different parts of the house.

The children only, were strangely unaffected – they didn't seem to hear any of the disturbances, continuing their conversations or their play in deep obliviousness to the thrashing or crashing sounds being heard by the adults. The only noises they were hearing, they said, was the lullaby sometimes at night. Soft and soothing it seemed to them, but far away.

They began to go hungry in the evenings though, soon after. When any food was put on the fire to cook, stones or bricks began to rain down on it. The chimney was examined, thoroughly, time and again. But no stone or brick was missing, and no cause or source of the damage was found.

As time went on the disturbances became worse, and Mrs. Kennedy (the younger) had to give up cooking food, as the time when cakes were being backed or pots were put to boil on the fire seemed to be the time of the most violent disturbances. Stones, mud, clay and sticks were pitched down on the food, and it could not be used.

At last William Kennedy, his wife, and his family, were forced to leave. There was nothing to be done for it – he began to look in earnest for a job and found a position outside of Wexford town that offered him bed and board for himself and his whole clann. Mrs. Kennedy (the younger) needed no convincing at that point, and away they went. She said afterwards though, that the most disturbing part of the whole affair was perhaps as they drove the cart away from the house on the last day, when they turned back and caught the children waving, to 'the woman of the house', they said.

So much were the people terrified by then, that the lawful owner John Kennedy (the younger) would not go to live in the house.

The whole place fell into ruins and there is no trace of it now, nor of anyone who used to live there.

50

An Bean Feasa

It's after taking me longer than I expected now, to get here. Dusk has fallen, and in the twilight I can see her lake, but I haven't a clue where the house is. I'm all turned around and the dark is coming in.

When I meet a man, he tells me her house is over that humpy bridge yonder, and up the hill. And so it is. And so here I am.

It doesn't look like anybody is home though. I'd heard she was dead, but then folk talk about her like she'll never die too, so it's hard to tell what's what. There's a door on the cottage, and I knock the door jamb. We'll see sure.

But it's a wee girl that answers. Looking up at me, she tells me that Biddy's dead and gone these long years, but she knows the stories, and would I like to hear some? I would indeed, says I, but where is her Mammy? Away, says she. Just, away.

Well.

We sit out in the drizzle and the damp, coz I don't want to go inside another one's home without their say so. The girl tucks in on the old stone wall, sheltered under the tree and wrapped in her long coat. I worry she's cold, but she says she's fine, and don't I want to hear some of the stories now? So shush, and listen.

"She had four husbands you know? And they all died of the drink, in one way or another. Sure she'd have 30 people coming to the house each day, the track must have been worn right down. But she'd never set a fee... just let people pay her what they had, and what they could. A lot of them brought the drink – a bottle of whiskey at least, but poitín too, and sometimes even the finest of wines. She'd take a bottle of finest claret or a spud from your garden, whatever you had to give was grand for her. So there was always drink in the house, and the husbands were into it. Even her last one, she married him at 71 and he only 30, and he didn't even last the year!"

"You don't say?" Says I, trying to imagine the match. I guess they were all wild ones she was with though, sure you'd have to be a bit to that side to be taking up with Biddy Early.

"Some say she went away with THEM, and that's where she got the knowledge of the cures and all she could do. But some others say it wasn't her at all that was away, but her brother, and that she went every night to a Fort to cry for him, til he came back and gave her the powers to keep herself to stall her grief. Other again say that it was a child she had, a wee one that would lie in the bed when she was around, but be up talking to folk in ways way beyond their years when she wasn't there, and with very old fashioned manners too. When the child went away she mourned it hard, and looked for it every day, so the powers were given to her to keep her busy and put her to work, so she'd leave Them alone on that subject.

Now, I know for a fact she didn't leave them alone, but used to go out to her garden and sit by this wall here, or into the shed that used to stand beyond it, and talk to Them all the time. And I know that her Mammy, whose family name she took though she was born of the Connors by her father, would dress her when she was only a child in fabric she wove from the flax of wild places, and she'd be off talking to Them from morning 'til night, and playing in the places they still live. I think maybe she earned the powers she had through her whole life... but those other things might be true either."

"That's fascinating", says I, marvelling at the child who seemed so wise way beyond her years, and most impressed by her lovely manners too. Please do carry on.

"The people do be full of stories of all the cures she did. It was by the bottle she did all, to shake it, and she'd see everything when she looked in it. Sometimes she'd give a little bottle of some cure to people that came, with herbs and other things inside in it, but it was a challenge to get it home safely. If she'd say to them - you'll never bring it home – well, break it they should on the way home, with all the care they'd take of it. But she kept her own big bottle safe with her, a one of blue green glass they say, and full of some dark liquid, or maybe nothing at all.

There was a man I knew living near the sea, and he set out to go to her one time. And on his way he went into his brother-in-law's house, and the priest came in there, and bid him not to go on. Well, Father, says he, cure me yourself if you won't let me go to her to be cured. And when the priest wouldn't do that (for the priests can do many cures if they like to, but they don't like to as it brings them closer to powers they don't want to be dealing with), the man went on to Biddy anyway. And the minute he came in; Well, says she, you made a great fight for me on the way, and he got the cure from her that day. For she could hear any earthly thing that was said in every part, even miles off. So they say."

And with that she gives me a nod, and a look I can't ever quite forget.

It's full dark now in the garden of Biddy Early, on the hill above the lake. There's no sign of the child's mother, but she assures me it's fine, and she'll go in to build up the fire and wait.

She looks cold though, and I give her my gloves - though they are too big for her delicate hands, they are warm wool and were made with love, and it is a small price to pay her for the stories she's shared.

That's not the only tale I can tell you of Biddy Early, An Bean Feasa –

the Wise Woman of Clare, for her legend lives yet in the hearts and minds of our people, and trips over tongues with only a little encouragement... but sure, they are all stories for another day.

51

Her and Her Bottle

The mass was finished, early enough thank god as the new young priest wasn't one for droning on with the gab like his predecessor. The usual crowd was rolling through the doors as Mikey polished some glasses behind the bar, and he said his hellos.

The pints were filled and the stout settled as the usual crowd started the usual oul shite talk, and Mikey was all set for a usual Sunday. But then the talk turned to a topic that did interest him, and his ears pricked up. They were talking about the witch above in Feakle.

Now, the Sunday crowd in Whitegate could absolutely be the ones to fill the air with nonsense, as the mood took them, but Mikey had noticed that every time her name came up, even in passing, there came on them a hushed manner, begob sure it was almost a… reverence, would ya call it? Whenever they spoke of her. Her and her bottle.

O'Leary, already on his second stout mind you, mumbled on something about the priest having heard about that bottle she had. The priest who lived near Biddy, it was, and he went to her and asked for the bottle, but she would not give him the bottle. He tried to take if off her, but he could not. No, says O'Leary, no way was he getting it. He was definitive enough now for a man who wasn't even there at the time,

Mikey thought, but he kept that to himself. Then when she died, her cousin wanted to get the bottle, but the priest had already gone and took the bottle, and threw it into a lake near her house.

Then a younger lad started talking, arra now Mikey couldn't even remember his name. But he could talk! And a bit fancier than the other lads too, it might have been an education had gotten into him at some stage in the game, and he still liked to show it off a bit, here and there.

"That noted witch in the parish of Feakle", says he, "had people coming from all parts of the country - especially Tipperary - to be cured." Did they have a higher than average illness rate in Tipp than in other counties, Mikey wondered? Or more of the Good Neighbours going round and about there? Again, those were thoughts he kept to himself, so he got back to listening to the lad talk.

No matter where you came from, he was saying, she called you by name coming up to her house. Two men were visiting her one night and they were drunk and they asked her to get a car to carry them home. "Sit into that carriage outside," said she. They did and were at home in a few minutes. The carriage disappeared and the two changed into mice and ran into a hole in the wall. Into mice lads... mice, if ya don't mind!

He'd another one on the go already though, and Mikey stopped his wondering and tuned back in to what was being spouted now.

Some four or five years ago, there was a big hurling match in Limerick, between Clare and Galway. Clare won. (This rose a ragged cheer from the assembled hurling aficionados.) The Galway hurlers were very mad and they called the Clare Hurlers by the name of that witch, and said they changed the colour of the ball in the field in order to gain the advantage and win it. She has a wide spread fame, even yet sure.

"I remember", pipes up oul Paddy from the corner stool - well, he was from Bodyke, actually, but the corner stool was where he was right then and there - "when I was in training 40 years ago to have said to me 'Oh you come from Biddy Early's place'. No fear I was complimented as coming from the Banner County who elected Daniel O'Connell! I said Biddy Early did not live in our parish, tho indeed she lived near the border of it. But sure none of them as was saying that woulda known it, nor ever been here."

There was much muttered commiseration with oul Paddy then, and Mikey didn't know if he was relieved or disappointed that the talk turned briefly to the greatness of O'Connell, and then wandered off into the more usual fallow fields of hurling. It both fascinated and unsettled Mikey Early to hear his ancestor being told of, and sure he never could decide which was the stronger feeling on it.

It's not the only time we've heard tell of Biddy and her bottle, mind you... but sure they're all stories for another day.

52

The Death Cry

The girl was walking home of an evening, long past twilight time, as she always did when her work at the big house was done.

Down the long drive, with the trees overhanging almost to touching each other in the branches above; like a tree tunnel, she often thought. The leaves had all but fallen off now though, the skeletal branches casting strange patterns as the moon shone down through them, and she quickened her step through the carpet of the discarded year, to get off their property and on down to the river, where she always felt more comfortable.

Many's the day she'd spent down on those banks, before the days were all taken with scouring and scrubbing up at the house. Just setting foot on the wee path that ran alongside the water gave her head some ease again, with the gentle gurgling noises making their way to her ears as she stepped light on the bare soil in the quickly deepening darkness that gathered as she walked. There was enough light to see by though, and the bridge was on up ahead. She knew it well enough to go by even when there wasn't a moon to guide by, and the one tonight was bright enough to light it all up sure.

Before she set foot on the oul bridge though, a cold wind blew up. It lifted her skirts and her hair, and she had the unsettling feeling it was blowing around inside in her as much as on the outside. She fancied she could feel it rattle round the hollow of her heart. The notion startled her, she wasn't usually given to such thoughts indeed, so she shook it off and stepped up onto the bridge, but she didn't yet have both feet placed on the cold stone when she saw there was an old woman crouched down, huddled in the shadows by the wall and rocking herself back on forth, faced away from the girl as she came on across the bridge.

Concerned, she called out - "Are ya alright, Seanmháthair?" Says she, but there wasn't even a hint that her voice had registered, or she'd spoken at all, from the poor oul crathure squatted there on the stone. She tried again - "It's a cowld night to be out in, Ma'am, have you any better lodgin' to go to now? Sure I can help you get there an all?"

No reaction.

But she did moan and rock and shake, like her oul heart was breaking clean out of her body, and it worried the poor girl so much she went to put a hand on the woman's shoulder, thinking maybe she was deafened, whether by birth or by grief. Getting closer though, as she reached out her hand, she began to see this being more clearly than the shadows had allowed for before, and it dawned on her that this was no more a woman now, than she was a cat.

Her hair was long, streelin down over her shoulders, and trailing a good yard out on the ground on either side of her. It was strong hair too, like you'd see on a young woman, a mad healthy lookin head of it and where it had looked grey before, she could see now - even in the washed out moonlight - that it was a mix and flow of a fox's ruadh and the bright silver echo of the moon on the river below. The dress now glimpsed under a worn grey cloak was deep green, and the cloak material like none she'd ever seen before; it ran over shapely arms the crathure had rested her head on, mingling with small braids and knots of hair as if they were lovers who couldn't bear to be apart.

"Go bhfóire dia orainn!" says she, in shock, and bedad wasn't it them very words that raised the head of the being before her, where none had worked before... and she saw for the first time what it was that truly sat in front of her on the bridge.

In a face as pale as the dead, with skin breac speckled and marked all across it, the eyes had a dead and alive look to them that drained all the warmth from her flesh as that gaze sought and found her own - they were the colour of forget-me-nots with none of the softness, as cold as the moon in a bog hole on a frosty night, and looking like they'd been sewn in with red thread, for all the crying that had been done through them.

And she knew. Even before the thing unfolded before her, arms outstretched and feet hanging above the good solid ground, rising to its full, towering height. Even before she got the proper look at the long hair that moved now with a life of its own, drifting and hovering around the flowing form. Even before the mouth opened and the soft grief moans she had been hearing escalated, rose to a wailing pitch and cry; a keen direct from the other world to this, that froze the blood in her veins and the marrow in her bones, and she was sure could be heard the next county over. Even before it turned away, gliding over the bridge and turning down towards the river, that awful cry lessening as it moved on upstream, melding and blending then with the noise of the water - gurgling and moaning becoming indistinguishable as the frozen fear receded and her mind began to work again.

It took a long time though - with the girl standing there unable to move, petrified on that spot but eventually she got the urgent message down as far as her legs, and they told her feet and her toes, and then they were all working well enough to carry her forward, picking up speed as she barrelled off the bridge on the other side, and away from the water, finding the forest path that led her home, launching her through the door, past her startled mother, and straight into her bed by the fire.

Diving under the heavy blankets and feeling their warm, comforting weight all on top of her, it calmed her body and soothed her mind.

Until her Mam came over that is, stripped the bedding off of her and demanded to know what in God's name was the matter with her?

She told the tale, of course she did, for her Mam knew well the ways of the Good Neighbours and was able to believe every word of it, having had a few such encounters in her own time on the land there.

So they talked, drank tea, cooked the dinner together and eventually went to bed... though she did find herself slipping into her Mam's bed for a cuddle and a comfort that eve, a thing she'd not done in a long while before or since, but they both understood that was ok. It had been an awful shock like.

And when they got the news, 3 days after, that the O'Brien had died down the way, sure neither of them were surprised. For wasn't their bloodline one of the five old families that the Bean Sidhe always showed up for?

That wasn't the first, nor the last time that Fairy Woman let her cry loose over the land of Ireland, warning of the death of one of the old blood... but sure, they're all stories for another day.

53

Reflections

"Why do they call you Danú, Lady? How have your own stories been lost so, and replaced by the ones from the mainland for all this long time?"

The cave interior was dim, even with the small fire lit inside in the hearth up the back, and the dappled light reflecting off the lake outside threw a faint blue tint on the skin of the large old woman sitting by the table right across from me. I knew from many years of visiting here, at all times of day and through all the year's cycle, that the deep water by the cave mouth, nestled in under the mountain peaks, could pick up and hold an amazing array of colours, from the land around and the sky above. But the one it loved to capture most was the brightest blue, and when it pooled most like crystallised cornflowers in the split of this grey green landscape, that was when her skin glowed blue within.

Long solid fingers, unfolded from around the cup from which she had been sipping our tea, and she looked to the cave mouth in silence, seeming to reflect deeply on my question before she formed her answer.

Her heavy skirts swished slowly then, as she rose to move past me, and settled carefully in the mouth of her cave there, as if to get a better look out at the lake. Maybe it gave her answers, or maybe she just liked the breeze off the water and the brightening blue tones lent to her as the light changed, and the sun shifted slightly toward its setting behind the valley.

I moved beside her, and waited.

There was never any point in rushing this one, she'd move at her own pace always, and it didn't do to rile her neither... the rest of us had learned that lesson well enough some long time ago.

"Arra sure, wasn't I their beantuathach all through anyway... what does it matter now?"

She spoke to me then of her birthing as Ana, of the mountain long ago. The people sang her stories and they brought their children to birth with her, and in her, and of her, and the ones who weren't strong enough to reach the sky became hers to keep.

And then was how I knew her, for weren't we sisters both, Great Queens and daughters of Earnmhas together? They call her the Mother of the Irish Gods, and she was indeed – a God and a Mother both. Of all of the Gods though? Not likely, no. Sure anyone who's had a look at that particular family tree knows well that it's not a single trunk with many branches. Isn't it more like a copse, or a grove, with all sorts of trees growing in it, of all sorts of ages and types, and some of 'em even grafted on or merging with one side by side, 'til you can't even really know which was the original or which tree to rightly call it, so you just have to accept it as a new thing altogether and appreciate it for what it is now? How could one single Mother birth and rear all of that on her own?!

A Mother of the Irish Gods, she is for certain, but not THE Mother. There isn't one.

"I am the mountain I sit under", says she to me. "They look for a neat box to put me in, but I am the very ground beneath their feet. I am the clay that holds the water, I shape the cup from which they drink. I hold the mothers safe, and bring the fathers to understanding how things work, in right order and right thinking, in honesty and honour, in love and life, and in living true to the land. I am the land on which they live, but they have forgotten me, Sister, before they began to forget you."

"Yet, now we rise", says I. "They hear our call, their lips murmur our songs once more. The know us, they fear us, they seek us out – for offering, for contract, for relationship. This world is turning once more, and the other world has not been forgotten. I send warriors and priests and worshippers, I send women to do the sacred work once more."

Ana's black eyes watched me, reflected and weighed my words, and then gave me a slight, slow nod of her heavy head.

"Yes, my Sister... Now we rise."

That's not the only time Herself has sought out conversations with her siblings and her peers... but sure, they're all stories for another day.

54

A Harvest Tale

She walked the roads.

From the first Spring falls, those light warm showers that woke the earth, she was out under the open skies again. Going nowhere, and everywhere. Watching, listening... taking it all in.

All the fresh new growth, the budding trees and blooming woodland colours. The freshening of each complexion she met, brightening eyes, quickly moving mouths eager to pass the time of day.

"Nach scéal leat?"

And so the stories would be told.

She walked the roads.

Byways and botharíns, trackways and toghers, courseways and cosáns.

Her hard feet fell on each surface and rose again, through bramble or bog she made her way, moving over the island from top to bottom, from one side to the next, wandering.

Walking the ways.

In the Summer she wore the name of Cailleach Feasa, and they would take advantage of the grand stretch in the evenings there to while away the longer hours with her in song or sounding, poetry, and even some light prophecy if she saw something in the signs around them. Often they'd prompt this by giving her a cup with strong green leaves and soothing tea so she could sup at her ease, but with a keen eye watch for the patterns that were made as the liquid was taken away inside her. Wise old woman was the name, or witch, or hag. But it didn't mean what you might think it means, in the now.

The dark of the night never bothered her. She'd find a hedge, or a deep ditch, or the boughs of a tree, or a thick bush, and take her ease within. Sometimes they'd find her with the first dawn light, and bring her some milk, or a bit of the cheese, and set her on her way again. Then through the day she'd bask in sunshine, or slip through the soft rain, stopping only when they asked her again, and again...

"Nach scéal leat?"

She walked the roads.

All through the light time of the year, on into the first chills as her weather turned towards summer's end. She'd savour the first shining fruit from the bramble - every time she popped that full dark shining gift between her thin lips, delighting in the sweet and tart mixture moving across her dry tongue at the very start of the harvest season, it would bring a smile to her purple stained mouth, and send her off on a hunt for more. Her sharp eyes watched the glistening greenery lining each little path, her body waiting for the swoop and dive she loved - even in this aged form – to pluck the blackberry from its safe nest and hook it to her eager maw, there to be devoured quickly.

And she'd watch the crops ripen in the fields. Wait as they tended them, and the sun took care of them, and the rain kept them growing and full.

And she'd hear their talk turn to her care through the dark time.

And she'd feel the small pinch each time, as they vied to be 'not it!', jesting and gesturing and jeering her age, her invalidity, her burden. None of them wanted to be left with the work of her for the Winter.

But, it was just the way of it. The way it always was, and ever had been.

In the Autumn, she wore the name of Cailleach Phiseogach, and they began to fear her as the darkness gathered beyond the horizon. As they cut and gathered they would shout to each other – "Have you put the hare out yet?" And they'd always leave the bit to last, the bit where the hare would shelter, til all else was done and they'd gather in to raise the noise, to put out the hare and send it on its way to the next one who'd be cutting and gathering. They'd laugh and slag on how they sent on the hare, so it wouldn't be their burden to bear.

Until the hare was left in the last field or garden, of the last family to cut or gather the last bit that needed the harvest.

She walked the roads.

She found her way there, to the last stand, and watched and listened and took it all in. The women stepped forth then, from the youngest to the oldest they went. Each casting an eye to where she waited as they took the cutting hook in their hands, each feeling the weight of their task, their responsibility, as they cast the hook to make the final cut.

And the one who did would be the one she went home with, and spent the darkness beside.

Together they walked the roads.

In the Winter, she wore no name. She walked with the woman and taught her the ways. The work was harsh, and went long. Long through the dark nights, running from the bright pinpricks of flame that dotted that landscape, deep into the depth of every dark work that had to be done. From the edge charm – ortha an fhaoir, to protective bobbins and ties for dwellings – human or not, to the healing of sickness inside and out – human or not, to the finding of the poor drowned souls and guiding them on – willingly or not.

But sometimes. Sometimes she'd get to sit.

By the warm hearth fires. In the cosy corner of a kitchen. Tucked under the eaves or rafters as the turf smoke curled lazily to the roof.

And as they'd come, they'd sit by her, or near her. So she'd get to gather, and ask them...

"Nach scéal leat?"

Have you any story?

55

For Ireland

Getting down on his arse in the grass under the hawthorn tree, the big man folded himself in ways that wouldn't have seemed physically possible to a casual onlooker moments before, and scooshed down into the dark and the mud.

Muttering and grumbling to himself about how they feckin wrecked a perfectly grand entrance, making it tiny and how was anyone of a good solid size even supposed to fit in there now... he dragged the cloth bag behind him, minding the contents as carefully as he could, as he made his way down, under the earth.

He could feel her strongly now.

The cries that had brought him to her echoed in his mind, searing deeply through his heart. She was not in this world, and he'd have to go through to the Other... down to the cave and up again, beyond the passage and down through the hall. He found his way easily - no stranger to her Ways was he - wending through tunnels, across open plains, seeking the source of the screams only he could hear. The wails that were digging and ringing and reverberating and resonating and scalding his spirit.

He carried the bag carefully, cradling the gifts he'd 'raided' from the lad who lived beyond down at the bottom of the island now, with his lass and their young one. The good rum, she liked that one. And the sandwich he'd made for her - with the good ham, bought from the deli counter in broad slices cut fresh from the slab of meat. The crumbed kind. The coleslaw, selected from the finest range for its creaminess and chunky veg. The one with the cheese in it. And last, but by no means least, the cheese itself. Grated mixture of red and white cheddar blending flavours and textures in a manner which is distinct yet mutually supportive.... Feckin hungry again now, so he was. Though he'd had 2 of the fine sandwiches himself at that point. He'd not touch hers of course, except to bring it to her. But damn if it didn't smell good.

Putting his rumbling tummy aside, he focused again on the call of his woman, and followed it on through 'til he found her.

Standing between earth and sky she was, in a place that blended both worlds again. He'd come full circle to a flat grey rock atop a tall mountain, surrounded with scrub and brush.

He made his way through and stood silently by her, and when she turned to him her mouth was open wide, a strong red scream echoing across the land. Her eyes were red fury too, and pain, and grief, and fear. Her hands were clawed and hooked, ceaselessly moving in ripping, shredding motions with her talon tipped fingers seeking purchase in flesh. Her red hair whipped wild about her head, alive with the energy and emotion that streamed from her, and to her.

She was in a cycle with the people who have been wronged. She keened and screamed and poured forth her venomous fury for Ireland.

For the past, and all that has gone before.

For those who have had to endure, have been cast aside or shamed.

For those who were hurt, or raped, or killed.

For those whose babies were taken, were stolen, were sold out from under them.

For those whose lives and deaths went unrecorded, unacknowledged, those who were hidden away in dark chambers beneath their 'holy ground', and the families who mourned them silently, uncomforted, alone.

For those who suffered everything for another's beliefs, whose pain and trauma was put to theoretical debate and wrongful judgement.

For Ireland.

Gently, he stepped towards her. Into the path of that terrible fury. He put out a hand, towards the rending, shredding one of hers. Her face turned to his and he felt it then, the full force of it turned on him and he shook under it. But he stood. Her eyes met his and with his own, he showed her silently that he was with her. No words, just witnessing. Just standing. Supporting, as he could. As she bore the weight of this, as she could.

And so she could stop.

Sinking to the grey stone, she put her head and her hands down to it, and she stopped. He felt the release of it, the relief of it. They both knew she'd have to take it up again, some time. And many times again, no doubt.

But for now, she could stop.

"They're making it change, Beloved. It's far from perfect, but there's plenty of them doing the work. On the island and off it, there's warriors walking their world who are bringing the change. Your change. I know you know it, but I wanted you to hear it."

When they turned to him again, her eyes were the Liath Grey of the rock beneath her, and calmer. Determined though, and fierce with it.

He shrugged, took her hand with one of his, and with the other he reached down for the cloth bag he'd carried to her.

"Here, I brought you something. Now, if you're not hungry, I'll be glad to take care of that sandwich. But there's the Oakheart rum you like in there too, I raided it for ya…"

That's not the only time Himself and Herself met at a certain time and a certain place, for a certain purpose... But sure, they're all stories for another day.[2]

---

[2] The Eighth Amendment of the Constitution Act 1983 changed the Constitution of Ireland, by inserting a subsection recognising the equal right to life of the pregnant woman and the unborn. Abortion had been subject to criminal penalty in Ireland since 1861; the amendment ensured that legislation or judicial interpretation would be restricted to allowing abortion in circumstances where the life of a pregnant woman was at risk. It was approved by referendum on 7 September 1983 and signed into law on 7 October 1983.

On 25 May 2018, a referendum was passed overwhelmingly to delete the constitutional ban on abortion, and at time of publication it is awaiting being signed into the law.

'For Ireland' was written on 27th May 2018.

About the Author

Lora is an Author, Teacher, and Guide: native born Irish, with 20+ years personal and professional experience in our history, heritage, archaeology, mythology, and pre-christian Irish Spirituality. Publications include - Irish Witchcraft from an Irish Witch, 2004; A Practical Guide to Irish Pagan Spirituality, 2013; Rathcroghan - a Journey, 2015; Tales of Old Ireland - Retold, 2018; and A Practical Guide to Pagan Priesthood, (Llewellyn) 2019.

She is a modern Draoí – a practitioner and priest of indigenous Irish magic and spirituality. Lora has been consciously following a Pagan path since 1994, and dedicated specifically to the Irish Goddess Mórrígan in 2004. She managed one of Ireland's most important sacred sites - Cruachán/Rathcroghan - for a decade, and is a co-founder and Reverend legal celebrant with Pagan Life Rites Ireland.

With her partner, Jon O'Sullivan (An Scéalaí Beag), she runs EelandOtterPress.net, and the IrishPaganSchool.com - an online learning environment where you can connect to the heritage, culture and spirituality of Pagan Ireland in an authentic and meaningful way, every day. Lora has 3 children, who are getting seriously grown up these days, and not enough animals or plants in her life to keep her happy.

Though she's not really one for a lot of responses to personal private messages - consider that your fair warning - you can find her in the comments section on her YouTube Channel content a couple of times a week, sending regular Irish Resources emails to her busy mailing list at LoraOBrien.ie, engaging with her Patron Members at Patreon.com/LoraOBrien, and personally moderating some very active community groups on Facebook; the Morrigan's Cave, Learn Ogham, Journeys in the Irish Otherworld, Do The Work System, and the Irish Pagan School Community.

You can connect with me on:
- https://loraobrien.ie
- https://twitter.com/LoraOB
- https://facebook.com/LoraOBrienInk
- https://irishpaganschool.com

Subscribe to my newsletter:
- https://lora-o-brien-irish-pagan-school.ck.page/67f96dd7b6

Also by Lora O'Brien

Would you like to receive a new story, just like these Tales of Old Ireland, each month?

Authentic Connection to Ireland
www.Patreon.com/LoraOBrien

Every month, Lora O'Brien creates a series of Irish Connection Rewards for the Patrons who support her on Patreon.

If you sign up to the $3 per month Reward level there, you too will be supporting a native Irish creator, and receive a fresh story for your 'Tales of Old Ireland' Reward – every single month.

Visit www.Patreon.com/LoraOBrien to learn more!

Rathcroghan: A Journey

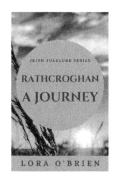

Authentic Connection to the Sacred Sites of Ireland

Lora O'Brien's work as an Irish Heritage Professional is about connection; to Ireland's history, mythology, ancestry, to the sacred and everyday sites. All of this is communicated and passed on through Ireland's stories.

This book is an expression of O'Brien's connection to 13 sacred sites of the Rathcroghan Royal Complex, in County Roscommon - home of Queen Medb and the Goddess Mórrígan - and the creative and intuitive inspiration that tells a story from each of those sites.

Over 25 years of exploring Irish Spirituality, Lora O'Brien has learned to connect, and to find the story.

Here she shares that experience with you - so you can join her, on a Rathcroghan Journey...

Buy it Now - https://www.amazon.com/Rathcroghan-Journey-Authentic-Connection-Folklore/dp/1722600535/

Introduction to Irish Paganism (Class)

Learn about Irish Paganism, Magic and Spirituality from a practicing Draoí, a Native Irish Priestess of Ireland.

- What do Irish Pagans Do?
- How Can I get Started in Irish Paganism?
- What can I do to Work with my Irish Ancestors?
- How do I connect to Irish Deities?
- How to Deal with the Other Crowd (the Good Neighbours, The Sidhe, the Irish Fairies)?
- What Offerings are Appropriate?
- What's the difference between Magic and Religion for an Irish Pagan?

This class includes 1.5 hours of structured teaching presentation, PLUS a Guided Journey to connect to Ireland directly – the land, the sovereignty, the Spirit of this Isle – using Lora's unique native Irish Otherworld Journeying method.

This class, and the Guided Journey, are suitable for beginners, as well as those with more experience in other traditions.

Learn More - https://irishpaganschool.com/p/pagan-intro

Join our Mailing List Community Today!

Get your Authentic Irish Resources, Information on Upcoming Classes (both free and paid) and Behind the Scenes Author News directly from Lora O'Brien.

Join Here - https://lora-o-brien-irish-pagan-school.ck.page/67f96dd7b6

Made in United States
North Haven, CT
02 October 2023

42279065R10125